W9-CYZ-263

RECEIVED
Institutional Research

DEC 1 1 1978

THE MANAGEMENT CONSULTANT

ALFRED HUNT, C.P.A.
RETIRED PARTNER, COOPERS & LYBRAND

A RONALD PRESS PUBLICATION

JOHN WILEY & SONS

New York • Chichester • Brisbane • Toronto

58719

Copyright © 1977 by John Wiley & Sons, Inc.

All Rights Reserved

Reproduction or translation of any part of this work beyond that
permitted by Sections 107 or 108 of the 1976 United States Copyright Act without the permission of the copyright owner is unlaw-
ful. Requests for permission or further information should be
addressed to the Permissions Department, John Wiley & Sons, Inc.

ISBN 0 471 07184-6

Library of Congress Catalog Card Number: 76–49741

PRINTED IN THE UNITED STATES OF AMERICA

10 9 8 7 6 5 4 3 2

658.403
H911m

58719

Preface

Despite the evidence to the contrary, many business executives feel that to employ a management consultant is a reflection on their own abilities. Employees often regard the arrival of a management consultant as inevitably leading to mass firings. Many young men and women just out of college, or knowledgeable in EDP, believe themselves prepared to be good and capable consultants.

Parallel with a general lack of understanding of the nature of the consulting profession is uncertainty in the public mind about its origins and development. As a certified public accountant who has devoted a long and active career to the practice of management consulting, I feel compelled to set the record straight.

Through this book I hope to make clear how consulting work began with the efforts of a few pioneering individuals, how its development followed that of the national economy, and how its period of greatest growth coincided with the unprecedented expansion of the public accounting profession and its rapid entry into the consulting field.

I hope also to convey a broad range of pertinent information about how consulting is practiced, who its chief practitioners are, what is required of a consultant and of a client, how consulting is practiced in foreign countries, and the future prospects of the profession in the United States and abroad.

Potential clients in business, government, and the non-profit sector should find facts and insights of value to them. It is also hoped that established practitioners as well as persons contemplating entering the profession will find the book interesting reading.

This book is dedicated to the clients for whom I have worked and to those associates who taught me to be a consultant and to those who were willing to learn from me. It is dedicated also to my wife and daughters who willingly joined in my extended visits to foreign countries and helped make it possible for me to acquire a broad spectrum of experience. Finally, I wish to recognize the efforts of my two Brazilian secretaries, Esther and Sandra, who greatly facilitated the production of the original manuscript.

ALFRED HUNT

New York, New York
September, 1976

Contents

	Introduction	3
1	What Management Consulting Is	6
2	Evolution of Management Consulting	13
3	Size of the Profession	21
4	The Management Consultant's Services	25
5	Types of Practitioners	30
6	Clients—An Overview	42
7	Selecting Clients	50
8	Finding the Right Consultant	59
9	How the Practice Is Carried On	69
10	Executive Search Engagements	101
11	Building a Consulting Staff	114
12	The Foreign Market	124
13	The Future of Consulting	137
	Appendix: Description of Specific Consulting Activities	143
	Index	155

THE
MANAGEMENT
CONSULTANT

Introduction

Mark Twain said, many years ago, "Everybody talks about the weather, but nobody does anything about it."

Now, I'm not going to claim that everybody talks about management consulting, but it seems obvious that nobody has done much of anything about explaining and describing this profession as it functions in its modern role of providing assistance to business, government, and institutions.

A few books have been written on the subject, and of the three major associations in the profession, two, the Association of Consulting Management Engineers (ACME) and the Institute of Management Consultants (IMC), have defined management consulting and produced brief tracts explaining it. The third, the American Institute of Certified Public Accountants (AICPA), has defined Management Advisory Services (which in many instances is identical with management consulting and will be considered so in this book).

But beyond this, I am not aware of any book that presents an overall point of view of the profession—how it originated, how it is carried on, and what its future holds. Therefore, the aim of this book is to provide such an overview. Not only so that management consulting may be better understood by the general public but also to help potential users of the service to better know how a management consultant can assist them, and, most important, to help young people choosing a career decide if this is the course they wish to follow.

Recently, when I was called upon by my firm to interview literally scores of young college graduates who wanted to get into this field without actually knowing very much about it, I came to believe that there was a pressing need for this type of book. And, upon further consideration, I came to believe that my almost twenty-five years spent full time in this work—with Booz, Allen & Hamilton; Haskins and Sells; and Coopers and Lybrand—superimposed upon audit experience with Peat, Marwick, Mitchell & Company and a stint as a plant controller for the Gillette Corporation, did, perhaps, qualify me to provide such an overview of the management consulting profession. What follows is my attempt to do so.

"Getting a handle" on consulting is not easy. Its scope of operations and the methods by which it is practiced vary from firm to firm, and even among offices of the same firm. To a large extent, consulting reflects the thinking, personality, and style of the practitioner. Its practice is largely unstructured. ACME, IMC, and the AICPA have all attempted to put some dimensions on the practice, but even they haven't been too successful. More recently, a senator in California introduced legislation that would set requirements for licensing management consultants. Many concerned parties, including the AICPA, claim that this is not advisable because such requirements are not needed and, additionally, some believe it is not possible to define the practice well enough to stipulate a common body of knowledge that a practitioner should master in order to meet the legal requirements proposed.

This prompts some people to ask whether consulting really is a profession. "After all," the question goes, "if it is not subject to regulations, and if it is possible for anyone to engage in it, providing he can find someone to buy his services, then why not call it a business like any other that provides useful personal services?"

Consultants usually reply by citing their years of specialized training and experience, their academic credentials, and the high standards of integrity and performance required by the professional societies to which they belong. It would be a mistake to equate the present lack of legislated certification requirements with a lack of stability in the practice of consulting itself.

In any case, the many years that the consulting profession has been in existence, the size of the profession, and the number of large and prestigious organizations using consultants certainly seem to indicate that the management consulting profession is here to stay, even though we can't neatly classify and package it. Nor does this book try to do so. This book is merely an attempt to introduce the reader to the management consulting profession, its practitioners, and their *modus operandi,* as I have encountered them—recognizing that there will be exceptions to almost every principle or norm mentioned.

In the chapters that follow, I provide some tentative definitions of consulting, and trace its origin, evolution, and growth. I describe the types of services provided, the practitioners who provide them, and the clients who receive them. Also included are chapters on selecting clients, selecting consultants, consulting and executive search procedures, the personal and professional characteristics of a good consulting staff, the foreign market, and, finally, a glimpse into the future of consulting.

1

What Management
Consulting Is

In describing a function, the first step is usually to define it. In describing management consulting (hereinafter called consulting), I therefore start with the definition given by the Association of Consulting Management Engineers (ACME), the first association of its type in the profession. ACME describes consulting as:

> . . . an organized effort by specially trained and experienced persons to help management solve problems and improve operations, through the application of objective judgment based on specialized knowledge and skill and systematic analysis of facts.

The organized efforts encompassed by consulting generally have extended themselves into, in broad general terms, three types of services. They are:

1. Providing an objective appraisal of existing conditions or plans;
2. Providing specialized technical knowhow that is not otherwise readily available to the client;

3. Providing assistance in carrying out a project, where the client does not have all the specialized talent needed.

All, or nearly all, types of consulting work will fall into one of these categories, and the client's need for these different types of services will vary in accordance with the particular conditions faced at any one time. A brief description of each of these services follows.

Objective Appraisal

Everyone realizes, I believe, how difficult it is to objectively appraise oneself. What is equally true but not so well known, perhaps, is that it is also extremely difficult for organizations to objectively appraise their own strengths and weaknesses. An outside, independent view by someone qualified to make such an appraisal is often required. This can be provided by the consultant.

An example comes to mind in the field of organization. In theory, the man at the top (president or chairman) ought to be able to objectively appraise his organization, and many of them do so. But to dispassionately appraise, in an informed, objective, and professional manner, such a vital thing as an organizational structure is often a task that, by its very magnitude and importance, justifies outside assistance. And this assistance is often provided by consultants who are expert in this field.

Within an organization there will often be differences of opinion among the top officers—as well there should be. If this never occurs, it indicates a potential weakness. Left to themselves, these officers can usually reconcile such differences, but often not satisfactorily. The argument can be won by the most persistent and most persuasive, which may not necessarily be the one who is right. Or the argument can be settled at the cost of producing antagonisms between men who, ideally, should work closely together every day. A consultant who is knowledgeable in the area under discussion can often provide guidelines to use in resolving such differences.

Another area requiring objective appraisal is that concerned with the development of important programs for the future. This includes such matters as long-range planning in a company, or a plan of action to carry out newly enacted legislation in government. Here, too, the task is frequently too great for management to carry out by itself, and too important to be delegated to subordinates. The use of a qualified consultant often provides for a rapid and more complete and objective development of a plan of action.

Often a client has decided on a course of action and has developed plans to carry it out, but he needs assurance and evidence that he has made the right decision and is in a good position to ward off or refute adverse criticism. In such cases, he may have consultants review his plans and either gain this assurance or else get recommendations for changes to improve his plans.

In this area, I recall several clients who asked us to appraise and document the adequacy of actions taken to control costs on construction projects totaling billions of dollars. At one point, I found myself in Vietnam evaluating the cost control efforts of a large contractor. This particular client was expecting strong criticism from our government because of some unfavorable publicity concerning the project, and he wanted to arm himself with an independent appraisal of his cost control procedures before the anticipated criticism materialized. In cases such as this, the supporting opinion of a knowledgeable and reputable consultant can be of immense aid and value.

Another area where the objectivity of the consultant is valuable is in cost reduction. Cost reduction is like military service—nearly everyone believes in it but few want to go through it. Many executives feel that costs in the other man's operations can always be reduced much more than in their own. However, a man from within an organization, even with top executive backing, will often be reluctant to exert force to reduce costs at the expense of incurring the ill will of his peers or superiors (unless he, himself, is very high in the organization structure). After all, this ill will may block his advancement at some time in the future.

The outside consultant does not have this fear, nor can he be accused of being partial to anyone in his recommendations. Moreover, he can sometimes suggest a new approach, different from that used in the company or even in the industry, which can provide significant opportunities for cost reduction.

Technical Knowhow

The earliest efforts in the consulting field were those wherein consultants provided clients with needed technical knowhow. The time and methods work of Taylor and Gilbreth are examples. More recent examples are the use of technical knowhow by consultants in developing and using the Program Evaluation Review Technique (PERT) in the Polaris missile program and in assisting clients to install computers.

In some cases, the client has the knowhow but this knowhow is vested in a busy executive who does not have time to use it or to train others to use it. And sometimes the client wants to embark on a program that requires, temporarily, more technically qualified people than he has available. Simultaneously installing new methods in many plants is an example. This can be done by the industrial engineering staff if it is large enough. If not, consultants can help to do the job.

Providing technical knowhow has always been a mainstay of the consulting profession. In early years it included the areas of industrial engineering, cost accounting, organization structure, and marketing. More recently it has included other areas: electronic data processing (EDP), management science, inventory control, environmental planning, and planning to minimize problems brought on by material shortages or cost increases.

The need of many companies to have ready access to knowhow that they do not have at all, or have in insufficient quantities, is a logical and continuing source of demand for the services of consultants.

Project Assistance

Sometimes a consultant is called upon to provide assistance to the client in carrying out tasks that are well within the capabilities of the client, but for which, because of the urgency or scope of the project, the client does not have the necessary staff. Given an adequate amount of time and expected continuation of this volume of work, the client can and should provide his own staff to do the work. However, in cases of urgency or in periods characterized by a shortage of trained and specialized people, the client will often call upon the consultant for what is known as project assistance.

This occurred to a very considerable extent during World War II and again during the Korean and Vietnam conflicts. As might be expected, project assistance during a war involves some bizarre aspects. In one instance in Vietnam, we had to reorder and arrange to have shipped by air essential goods that were already on a ship in the harbor—the ship could not be unloaded for another month or two!

The need for this type of consulting work occurs frequently in government. The passage of new legislation often opens up a whole new program of action, which the government agency does not have the staff to handle. This has occurred very extensively in the Department of Health, Education and Welfare, which has been given greatly expanded areas of operation in all three of its major activities.

The costs of staffing up to meet the temporary demand for services are often quite large because of the need to recruit and train, and subsequently terminate, people. Using consultants for this type of operation normally is not significantly more expensive, and it is usually more expeditious. This type of project assistance rarely appeals to consultants, who take pride in genuinely challenging work. However, in that it serves a real need, particularly in times of national emergency, it does have its place in the scheme of things.

The demand for project assistance from consultants stems largely from three sources: national emergencies, enactment of new laws and regulations by the government, and the dynamics of enterprise (i.e., the fact that all enterprise is so dynamic, so changing, that there is no stability—people talk about a *status quo,* but it only lasts for an instant). Each of these can produce a need to perform, in a vastly expanded manner, functions normally carried out by the client.

On the other hand, in a period of economic recession a client will attempt to maintain his work force intact and will normally try to do as much work as he can with his own staff, instead of using consultants. This is one of the reasons why the volume of consulting work is subject to significant fluctuations, depending upon the health of the economy. The significant downturn in the volume of consulting work during 1970 and early 1971 was evidence of this.

*   *   *

In this chapter I have attempted to describe, in very general terms, the nature of consulting work, why and how it is used, and the factors that affect its volume. With this general understanding of the profession, it is possible to better understand and appreciate the forces that have influenced the evolution of consulting, which is the topic of the next chapter.

2

Evolution of Management Consulting

Consulting, in the sense that I am writing of here, is almost 100 years old. It began in the United States around the turn of the century, and was carried on by men whose names are still bywords in the profession. Taylor, Emerson, Gilbreth, and Gantt are outstanding examples of the consultants who played major roles in starting the profession.

These men brought to the factory a scientific approach. They questioned existing methods and were courageous enough to suggest completely new techniques in manufacturing operations. Their dedicated and all-pervading approach toward improved productivity was vividly depicted in the book *Cheaper By The Dozen,* written by the daughter of Frank and Lilian Gilbreth. (I once heard Lilian Gilbreth relate an anecdote that perfectly illustrated her husband's dedication to his profession. It seems that one day as Frank lay sick in bed, a painter began painting the house. Through the window Frank heard him whistling " 'Way Down Upon the Swanee River" in time with his brush strokes. Frank turned to Lilian and said "Tell him to whistle 'Dixie,' instead.")

When one looks at a picture of a factory of those days, it is easy to realize the innumerable opportunities that existed for methods improvement and for improving compensation through increased productivity. I can refer old-timers, at least, to their memories of a newspaper cartoon "Out Our Way," which pictured grizzled mechanics in oversized overalls walking around with tools hanging out of their pockets. (The cartoonist knew his subject well, for he had worked in a machine tool works where some colleagues and I developed, in 1952, the first management information system that I had ever heard of. I thought we had coined the term.)

Thus, the first consultants worked in factories and specialized in improving work methods and in setting time standards for production work. As time went on, however, business, industry, and government sought assistance from consultants in many other areas, and the consulting profession grew. This growth was marked by a number of milestones, as I shall discuss below.

World War I

In the early days of the century, factories used great amounts of labor, since they were largely unautomated. The rapidly increasing demand for manufactured products that occurred during World War I spurred the growth of unions and a resulting demand for higher wages. These conditions, coupled with the then marginal standard of living of the average factory worker, provided a fertile field for the improvement of work methods and the establishment of time standards and incentive compensation systems.

World War II

Throughout the depression years, consultants had difficulty in obtaining engagements, as most companies had cut their operations to the bone and had little money to spend for consultants. However, World War II changed all that. Beginning with our aid to England and France, and our own efforts to prepare ourselves before our entry into the war, there came a welcome demand for the products of our industrial machine. During this period, as we developed an armed force of 12 million men, we had a tremendous shortage of labor and had to recruit untrained workers for our industrial work force. Most of these people were completely unfamiliar with factory operations. These conditions provided a great opportunity for consultants to improve factory operations, resolve production bottlenecks, and develop methods and programs to train new workers.

Also at that time, there was plenty of money available to pay for consultants. Many government contracts provided compensation on a cost-plus basis, and companies were faced with an excess-profits tax on earnings significantly above those of the pre-war period. Both of these factors led to the expanded use of consultants, because, in effect, the government was paying for a large portion of their fees, either through higher costs or through foregone taxes. However, the consultants, themselves, were faced with the problem of finding adequate staff to man this ever increasing volume of work placed at their doorsteps. Their ability to surmount this obstacle is a tribute to the ingenuity of the profession.

Korean War

The Korean war provided a similar opportunity for consultants, although in a less dramatic fashion. Here again, manufacturers were working on cost-plus contracts for the government and were faced with an excess-profits tax. Consulting costs were considered an expense in the year in which they were incurred. Therefore, they tended to reduce profits and produce an almost corresponding reduction in the income taxes of a manufacturer faced with an excess-profits tax. To the extent that the manufacturer gained lasting benefit from improvements made to his company by consultants, this was a benefit to him which, in effect, was largely paid for by the Federal Government. Therefore, astute business managers used these tax-financed services as a springboard to profitable and expanded operations during the war and post-war periods.

And once again, there was a significant increase in the demand for consultants. But this time, the consulting firms had fewer staffing problems. They had already built up sizeable staffs as they assisted American industrialists in converting to peace-time operations after World War II and in preparing to expand their operations overseas. (These larger staffs were somewhat shaken in 1953, however, when Congress repealed the excess-profits tax. In fact, the managing partner of one major firm felt compelled to call a meeting at that time to reassure the staff that "everything won't go to hell in a handbasket when the tax expires.")

Cold War

Following the Korean War and the Berlin blockade, the United States entered the Cold War period. This gave rise to a significant and continuing expenditure for military preparedness and to cost-benefit analyses aimed at determining which of the various alternative weapons systems to employ. These efforts stimulated the use of what is now referred to as management science in arriving at solutions to these difficult problems. PERT was developed to expedite the development and production of the Polaris missile, and Critical Path Method of scheduling military contract work became a required part of contracts with the Department of Defense. The use of mathematical techniques in short-term forecasting and in inventory control, and the use of sensitivity analyses and capital budgeting techniques became common. The volume of expenditures for this type of effort, directly or indirectly paid for by the Federal Government, led to the establishment of government-sponsored mathematical and management science types of research organizations, often referred to as "think tanks."

Coincident with this development in the public sector was the decision by many large U. S. companies to locate production facilities overseas, particularly in Europe. This was done to tap the foreign market, which could not be satisfied to any great extent by U. S. production because of the strength and scarcity of the dollar and resulting high prices for U. S.-made goods sold in the foreign market. As these U. S. companies went overseas, they wished to take with them the manufacturing, marketing, and organizational techniques that they had successfully employed in the U. S. To assist them in this, they called upon consultants, who helped them to lay out plants and establish working methods and time standards. Consultants also helped in market studies and in developing marketing organizations and plans, as well as in overall corporate long-range planning. This provided a firm base for the overseas operations that today account for about 20 per cent of the billings of management consulting firms as a whole.

Moving overseas prompted management consulting firms to open offices in the major capitals of Europe, South

America, and the Orient. Consulting work done by CPA's in foreign operations was done largely through established offices in those countries, either operated directly by the U. S. firm or in connection with English or other firms operating in these countries.

The Computer Era

The introduction of the computer marked a new era for consultants. The process of selecting and installing a computer required an expertise that most companies did not possess. To meet this need, consultants added to their staff people knowledgeable in the computer field. Some were former systems engineers or salesmen for the computer companies, and others were consultants specifically trained by the firm in this area. The ability to install similar systems in companies within the same industry provided a great opportunity for consultants to transfer their know-how in computers from one company to another.

Because of the considerable effort needed to program computers, this work was also often contracted out by the computer user. This led to the development of "software houses," companies who programmed computer applications. Initially, these programs were custom designed to meet the needs of a specific client. From there, these software houses moved into producing general-purpose computer programs that could be marketed to a number of computer users. The software houses also expanded into systems development work related to the computer, and became a significant entity within the consulting field.

With the advent of computers, the forging of management science into a management tool also became increasingly important. The use of mathematics to solve business problems in the areas of production scheduling, inventory control, production, distribution, financial planning, and capital budgeting increased tremendously. Developing mathematical models to use in future planning became an accepted practice.

These techniques lean heavily on the use of computers to carry them out, and, to make computers more accessible, time-sharing terminals permitting the use of a computer by many people at points remote from the computer were developed and installed. Here again, consultants assisted in introducing these management science techniques into client organizations and in developing, installing, and using the time-sharing networks needed to carry out management science activities.

During this same period, government programs were permitted to expand significantly into areas where they had never penetrated very deeply before. Prime examples were the social programs in the fields of health, education, and welfare, and, more recently, areas such as transportation and criminal justice. Large appropriations were made by Congress to carry out new programs in these areas, and these appropriations were often funneled through Federal agencies into state or local governments. As a result, these Federal, state, and local agencies were faced with the need to develop and carry out new programs on a large scale.

Medical assistance, student education, aid to the indigent, and community action units designed to foster economic equality for the disadvantaged were major features of these programs. Everything, from assistance to local police forces in apprehending criminals and bringing them to trial to surveys aimed at the development of mass transportation and assistance in developing such systems, became major fields of endeavour. These activities were, in most instances, beyond the capabilities of the respective governmental units to carry out without assistance. So these units turned to the consultants for help, and this, too, became an important field of work for the consulting profession.

* * *

This chapter has provided a thumbnail sketch of how consulting grew and developed, and the factors that influenced this growth and development. It is now in order to take a look at the magnitude of the consulting profession today. This is the subject of the chapter that follows.

3

Size of the Profession

During the first 50 years, most consulting work was done by consultants or consulting firms who devoted their time exclusively to this type of work. However, in the '50's and early '60's, more and more certified public accountants began to recognize opportunities to participate in consulting work. This was particularly true of many of the larger firms.

CPA's had always been called upon for advice by their clients, initially on accounting matters, then on taxes, and then on Securities and Exchange Commission registrations. Thus, clients had become used to calling upon their CPA's for counseling and guidance. The natural confidence that the client had in his CPA made it easy for him, in most cases, to consider the CPA as a good source of consulting assistance, although some of the larger client companies had difficulty in bringing themselves to acknowledge that the firms that had formerly operated only in a financial capacity were now equipped to render counsel and guidance in areas such as production, marketing, and organization. Today, a very significant part of consulting work is being done by CPA's.

In addition to the CPA's, another group of professionals entered the consulting field. These were people from colleges and universities, both professors and students. This movement was prompted by a number of factors. First, teachers wanted to gain practical experience to make their teaching more productive, and providing consulting assistance in the areas of their teaching specialties was a logical way of doing this. Associated with this was the desire and need for teachers to publish—and practical experience in implementing theory was a valuable aid to a teacher in producing more substantive writing.

The size of the consulting profession today is somewhat difficult to determine. The profession is highly unstructured, and it is hard to decide who should be considered a consultant and who should not. Even if we use the previously mentioned ACME definition of management consulting:

> . . . an organized effort by specially trained and experienced persons to help management solve problems and improve operations, through the application of objective judgment based on specialized knowledge and skill and systematic analysis of facts.

we have trouble deciding who is doing consulting work.

A retired businessman working in a foreign country and receiving only money to cover his expenses is providing consulting services. A man who audits freight bills probably is not, even though he might call himself a traffic consultant. Large consulting firms with executive search services will usually consider such services as consulting; whereas firms who do nothing but executive search are not usually considered to be doing consulting.

Even within the "Big Eight" of the AICPA, some firms classify certain types of advice given to their clients as management advisory service, whereas others classify as management advisory service only work performed on a project basis by their MAS division. For example, some firms classify their actuarial departments as MAS, while others do not. Thus, the problem of deciding who is doing consulting work, and therefore who is a consultant, makes any estimate of the size of the profession somewhat uncertain. Nevertheless, with Philip W. Shay of ACME as my chief guide, I will attempt to penetrate the maze of available statistics and give some idea of the size of the consulting profession today.

Mr. Shay estimates that there are about 3,500 consulting firms operating in the United States in 1975. The vast majority of these are small firms of two to five men each, with less than 150 firms serving clients on a broad range of problems. He also estimates that the number of individuals doing consulting work today is close to 60,000. Of these, some 8,000 are employed by CPA firms, some 40,000 are employed by independent consulting firms, and between 8,000 and 10,000 practice on their own. (Each of these types of practitioners is discussed in some detail in Chapter 5.)

Mr. Shay further estimates that the independent firms grossed $2,000,000,000 in 1970, while the CPA firms grossed an additional $500,000,000. The two largest independents, Booz, Allen and Hamilton and McKinsey and Company, grossed $49,000,000 and $45,000,000, respectively. The third, fourth, and fifth largest providers of consulting services, who averaged over $30,000,000 each in yearly billings, were all CPA firms, according to the trade publication, *Consultants News*. No figures are available for the equivalent fee values produced by the internal, or in-house, consulting units located in an estimated 800 U.S. companies.

Altogether, no matter how it is measured, consulting is big business. It has grown rapidly from just fifteen consulting firms in 1910, to the present 3,500 firms. There have been only a few periods when this steady growth has been slowed or temporarily reversed, the most recent occurring in 1971 and early 1972. With the resumption of growth in 1973, many firms are now anticipating a 10 to 15 per cent yearly increase through 1980. The future growth of the profession is considered in greater detail in Chapter 13.

* * *

With that brief look at the size of the consulting profession as it stands today, in the next chapter we turn our attention to the types of consulting services offered by these 3,500 consulting firms.

4

The Management Consultant's Services

As indicated in my earlier comments, the range of services provided by consultants is very broad. In fact, the only limitations that exist are those determined by what clients have a need for. As matters stand today, the consulting environment is a striking example of the free enterprise system and leaves it up to the consultants themselves to determine the range, nature, and quality of the services provided by the profession.

Generally, however, the range of services performed by any consultant or consulting firm is closely aligned with the skills of that man or firm. Some of the large ACME firms have performed a wide range of (management) consulting services. Other firms tend to specialize in more restricted areas of the market. CPA firms, for example, generally have emphasized engagements relating to the financial area. Some firms have specialized in industrial engineering, or marketing, or materials management types of engagements.

The following schedule provides a more complete picture of the consulting activities that comprise the bulk of the practice. This schedule lists the functions and the specific consulting activities pertaining to each. A description of each of these activities is also contained in the Appendix.

Function	Specific Consulting Activities
General Management	Organization studies
	General surveys
	Long-range planning
	Top management appraisal
	Executive compensation
	Executive search
Production	Plant layout
	Production methods
	Time studies
	Production scheduling
	Inventory control
	Materials handling
	Equipment maintenance
	Plant safety
Marketing	Market analysis
	Sales forecasting
	Distribution methods
	Sales compensation
Finance	Accounting systems
	Cost accounting systems
	Budgeting systems
	Cash forecasting
	Financial feasibility studies
Personnel	Job evaluation
	Wage and salary administration
	Personnel record-keeping
	Staff training
	Labor relations
EDP	Computer surveys
	Feasibility studies
	Equipment selection
	Systems development
	Computer programming
	Computer scheduling
	Employee training

Function	Specific Consulting Activities
Cost Reduction	Systems analysis Work simplification Work measurement Incentive compensation

Special Services	Management science:
	  Training
	  Applications
	Telecommunications
	Environmental controls
	Transportation:
	  Analysis
	  Scheduling
	Resource utilization

Specific conditions existing at any one time will largely determine the extent to which various types of consulting activities will be in demand. Essentially, there are four factors that dictate the type of service that may be in demand at any one time:

Changes in the economic cycle,
Stages of the client's growth cycle,
Changes in the availability of resources, and
Changes in laws and regulations.

Changes in the economic cycle affect not only the volume but also the type of consulting work to be done. During a period of economic prosperity, clients will normally be more interested in organization studies, market analyses, executive compensation, executive development, and executive search. During the down-cycle, companies are apt to be more interested in cost reduction and economic planning and control.

The type of services that the client will need will also depend on the degree of maturity of both the client company and the economic society in which it operates. A new company will be much more interested in services dealing with producing and marketing its products than in executive planning and development or organizational reform. Similarly, industries in a young, growing nation will be much more production-oriented than those in a less dynamic, more mature economy. For example, in Brazil today, a great amount of work is being done to install modern production and management methods in industry.

Changes in the availability of resources will produce opportunities for consulting work. Currently, because of the high costs of fuel, a number of consultants are counseling clients on how to minimize fuel consumption through better maintenance, scheduling, and dispatching of motor vehicles. Periods of scarcity of human resources will lead to engagements to assist clients in reducing the amount of labor required to produce a product or service. The present interest by retailers in point-of-sale recording equipment to automatically read and record prices and stock numbers of articles sold has provided an opportunity for consultants to counsel and guide retailers in the selection and installation of this type of equipment. The need for this equipment is prompted not only by the desire to provide better control of inventories and more accurate "ring-ups," but also, and even more so, by the cost of competent help to man check-out stations in supermarkets and other retail stores.

Changes in laws and regulations will produce accompanying changes in the demand for consulting services. The present emphasis on environmental control has produced a spate of engagements to assist companies in eliminating air and water pollution. Similarly, the government's emphasis on health care has greatly expanded the demand for consultants to assist in the health care field. And the greatly increased government expenditures for criminal justice have brought significant opportunities for work with local police departments and with regional and national data processing systems used to aid in the prevention of crime and apprehension of criminals.

In summary, the consulting profession provides a very wide range of services to clients. The range is so wide as to preclude all but the largest firms from providing the full range of services. Generally, each firm will specialize in a few areas, determined largely by the skills of those in charge. Demand for services will be dictated largely by client needs at any particular time, and will vary according to economic conditions, the client's stage of development, and external factors such as the availability of resources and changes in laws and regulations.

*   *   *

With this knowledge of the breadth of the profession and the factors that influence it, it is natural to wish to know more about the people who provide consulting services. This is the subject of the next chapter.

5

Types of Practitioners

Having just reviewed the types of services that consultants perform, it now seems appropriate to discuss the types of practitioners who perform those services. I will begin by classifying practitioners in terms of the end products they produce. In broad general terms, these end products are: (1) information and/or systems, and (2) people.

The practitioners whose end products are information and/or systems provide, by far, the largest amount of consulting assistance and earn the major portion of consulting revenue. These practitioners can be further classified into seven groups as follows:

Management consulting firms:
  ACME
  Other
CPA firms
Academicians
Sole practitioners
In-house consultants
Software firms
EDP equipment manufacturers

Each of these types of practitioners is discussed separately below, and I will then discuss the practitioners whose end product is people (i.e., executive search firms).

Management Consulting Firms

Management consulting firms themselves are of essentially two types—ACME and other. Most of the large firms and some of the smaller firms are members of ACME.

Chief among the large firms are McKinsey & Co., A. T. Kearney, Fry Consultants, A. D. Little, and Booz, Allen & Hamilton. These firms employ from 200 to possibly over 1,000 consultants, and their services cover a wide range of activities. Some, such as Booz, Allen & Hamilton, have become corporations and sold stock to the public. Their annual financial statements and the registration statements that they were required to file with the Securities and Exchange Commission provided an insight into the volume and profitability of these companies. However, Booz, Allen & Hamilton is now privately held and information on their operations will not now be so readily available. Other large firms, such as McKinsey, are still privately held corporations, and not as much is known about their activities.

The smaller firms are generally those with two to five, or possibly ten, partners or owners who usually specialize in a specific area of work. Some have tended to specialize in top management and marketing areas. Others have concentrated on materials handling, cost reduction, etc. Some of these firms have been in business for a long time. Others have sprung up—some to flourish and subdivide into other companies and appear under new names, and others to go out of existence when their backlogs of clients and work are exhausted. In their particular specialties, these small firms are quite effective. Some of them are members of ACME and some are not. They are usually headed up by dynamic individuals who know how to analyze situations and how to motivate people. Taken together, these firms perform a significant volume of consulting work.

Among the non-ACME firms are some captive firms— consulting firms that have been acquired by conglomerates and have not proved to ACME that they are professionally independent. Those firms that have been able to successfully provide this proof have been allowed to remain in, or be readmitted to, ACME.

A prime example is Cresap, McCormick and Paget. This firm like many others such as Fry Consultants and numerous executive search firms, is an off-shoot of Booz, Allen & Hamilton. Cresap, too, went public and was later acquired by the First National City Corporation, the holding company that owns the First National City Bank of New York.

The acquisition of CMP by First National City Corp. caused considerable concern among other member ACME firms, who alleged that in its new subordinate position, Cresap could no longer be considered truly independent. They argued that Cresap was an arm of the bank, and that its findings in its consulting work could be communicated to bank lending officers, thus constituting a breach of the confidential relationship that should exist between consultants and their clients. On this basis, they voted to take away from Cresap its membership in ACME.

Some observers, however, believed that the ACME firms were more afraid that Cresap would gain an undue marketing advantage because it was allied with a large bank, and they feared that lending officers of First National City, when suggesting consultants to customers, would be required to recommend Cresap and thus deprive other

ACME firms of this potential source of business. Nevertheless, ACME has since reversed itself and readmitted Cresap to membership, and it appears that Cresap will continue to be a force in the profession. However, it is more difficult to determine Cresap revenues and profits now that it is part of a conglomerate. Perhaps the product line reporting regulations required by the Securities and Exchange Commission will ultimately shed more light on the activities of Cresap and other captive firms.

CPA Firms

As indicated earlier, CPA firms, although arriving late, have become a sizeable factor in the practice. It is estimated that, taken together, CPA firms do approximately 20–25 per cent of the total consulting work being performed. In any list of large firms in terms of revenue and numbers of professionals, there are two or three CPA firms among the top ten.

The CPA's have had many things going for them as they have entered consulting work. One important advantage is the continuing relationship that each CPA firm has with its audit clients. In many cases, these relationships extend back over 20 to 50 years, during which time these CPA's have gained the confidence of their clients in the integrity and quality of their services. Moreover, CPA's have long been giving advice to clients; tax advice, financial planning for executives, assistance in obtaining financing for the company, and obtaining or recommending financial officers are examples. These are important considerations when we realize that practically all large companies require audits, and, therefore, there is a CPA firm close to every such company.

A second advantage is that, as they entered the consulting field, CPA firms were already well equipped with offices and top management talent. The large national

CPA firms had offices throughout the U. S. and in foreign countries, and thus were strategically located to provide consulting services, and, more importantly, the local contacts to help in obtaining work. Also, having been in business a number a years and having a large, going operation, CPA firms had the money necessary to enter into consulting work and to finance large engagements. Thus, with the exception of professional consulting talents, the large CPA firms already possessed before-hand most of what was needed to enter the field.

As the large CPA firms and some of the smaller ones entered consulting in a formal manner, numerous small CPA firms and private practitioners were providing and continued to provide consulting assistance to clients in an informal manner. Setting up accounting systems, recommending controllers, assisting in relations with bankers, and advising clients when to sell shares of stock in their companies were all practiced by these CPA's as a matter of daily routine.

Often, these smaller firms of CPA's, when making the annual audits, had recognized the opportunity to assist the client to improve systems and would arrange to do this work during the summer season when the work of auditing was at a lower level. No one knows exactly how much consulting work has been done by CPA's in this manner, but many believe that in total it constitutes a significant amount.

Academicians

Another group of practitioners has come from the colleges and universities, as certain professors, particularly those in schools of business administration, have moved into the consulting field.

Their consulting work is carried on in a relatively informal manner. The professor, being a man of status in his community, has contacts with top business leaders. His knowledge and insight into business problems, and the thought he has given to them, interest business executives faced with these problems. In other instances, former students of these professors have come to them with specific problems. Often, professors will use graduate students to assist them in their consulting activities. This is good experience for the graduate students and provides an excellent source of manpower to the professor.

Generally, professors will take on engagements at a much lower hourly rate than that charged by established consulting firms. Professors have no significant overhead and they have a steady income from their teaching work. Thus, in terms of price, they can be formidable competitors to established consulting groups. However, because consulting is not a full-time occupation, each professor cannot, individually, do a significant amount of work, and, thus, sizeable projects that need to be completed quickly are usually given to full-time consulting firms.

Occasionally, recognizing the potential in certain areas in which they are specifically knowledgeable, professors have left their universities and have formed their own consulting groups.

Sole Practitioners

There are countless sole practitioners in the profession. Some of these do not even have an office. The name of their company is usually the practitioner's name, followed by "& Associates." The associates are usually whomever he might hire for any particular engagement.

Sometimes a man becomes a specialist in the field in

which he is working and feels that he can earn more advising others than he can working for his employer. So he will either leave and set himself up in practice as a consultant, or he will carry on this type of consulting on a part-time basis. Many accountants in private industry act as consultants to small companies on accounting and financial matters.

A third group of people who do solo consulting are the people who are between jobs. These are often men who have held important positions in specialized fields of industry. For one reason or another, they may have lost or resigned these positions and are using consulting work either as a stepping stone to a permanent practice or as something to tide them over until they find permanent employment. A good position will often tempt them to give up their consulting practice for steady, dependable income.

In-House Consultants

Another group of consultants is composed of in-house consultants—people who are employees of a large company and who work exclusively for that company. Some large companies, such as General Electric, have established in-house consulting groups specifically for this purpose. Top managements of these large companies, having seen the large amount of money being paid out in consulting fees, have decided that this work can be done more cheaply by company employees, thereby eliminating some of the overhead and the profits that would normally be included in the fees paid to outside consultants.

These in-house consultants work in much the same manner as outside consultants. They are usually invited in by the head of an operating division of the company and given a specific problem to solve. This operating division is charged for the fees of the consulting group.

In some cases, the head of the in-house consulting group must move throughout his company to find an opportunity to market his services. In other cases, services of this group are recommended by top management to assist operating managers in solving their problems. And in still other instances, these in-house consultants may be sent into a division or department by top management to work for top management in investigating conditions existing there.

In general, working at a medium-to-lower level of operations, these in-house consultants can do a good job. Often they have basic talents roughly equivalent to those of consultants in outside firms. In fact, many of them are recruited from outside firms. These in-house consultants usually know their company's operations well, and, equally as important, they know the philosophy underlying these operations.

However, when in-house consultants begin to operate at the higher levels of management they are usually not so effective. As mentioned earlier, many of them cannot be completely free in their recommendations because of their reluctance to offend executives in the company who may, at some future date, have a say in their advancement. Secondly, there is the problem of lack of objectivity, or "not being able to see the forest for the trees." These people have become so deeply ingrained with the philosophy that certain actions are *always* taken in this company or in this industry that they see no reason to question them.

With the growth of conglomerates, in-house consultants became more numerous. Now that the formation of conglomerates seems to have subsided somewhat, in-house consultants may not continue to increase so rapidly. However, they will always be a factor in the profession.

Software Firms

A new force in the market has been the software consultants. These are companies initially formed to develop custom-made computer programs for systems being developed by individual companies. This became a very large market, since many companies did not have the staff needed and did not wish to staff up to do the work of developing all the programs needed to initially install a computer.

As these consultants began developing programs to meet the needs of specific companies, they recognized that with small modifications many of these programs could be sold to other companies. Thus, they began developing standard computer program packages covering specific activities, such as inventory control, payroll, and accounts receivable and payable. This gave them the opportunity to market their products to a wide range of companies that were installing or using computers, and this led to the opportunity to do systems work, as well, for many of their clients.

In addition, computer manufacturers turned to these software houses for the operating programs that were needed for their computers. Most major computer manufacturers have gone outside to computer programming companies to obtain the operating system programs needed for their third and fourth generation computers.

EDP Equipment Manufacturers

A still more recent entry into the consulting market has been the EDP equipment manufacturers. For many years, EDP manufacturers provided systems help to their customers as a service that went with the price paid for the computer. Computer manufacturers wanted to be sure that customers used their equipment properly, particularly because it was rented rather than sold and could be returned if not satisfactory. Therefore, they provided the systems help needed to get the computer operating satisfactorily.

IBM was the leader in this practice. Its well entrenched position in the industry gave it the resources needed to provide this assistance, and it was often a major factor in the decision by a user to acquire IBM equipment instead of another make. This advantage became so pronounced that the Federal Government forced IBM to charge separately for this service.

IBM then went one step further. Not only did it provide systems help directly connected with installing computers, but it also provided systems help in other areas. Some major systems jobs, such as the one to develop the automatic fare collection system of the Bay Area Rapid Transit System in San Francisco, resulted from this decision.

Here again it is difficult to know the volume of work that is being done in the systems field by computer equipment manufacturers, because these figures are buried in the overall revenue figures of these computer companies. Perhaps the full disclosure of revenue and profits by product lines mentioned earlier will provide this information.

Needless to say, if their services are properly marketed, the computer manufacturers should be able to develop a significant amount of consulting work through the close connections established with customers by computer salesmen as they service existing computer installations or attempt to sell new ones.

Executive Search Firms

The end product produced by executive search firms is people rather than information or systems. Typically, the executive search firm undertakes to find an executive for a specific top or middle management position in the client organization.

Executive search firms may be of two types: those that perform only executive search and those that perform other functions as well. The other functions may be the whole range of management consulting services of a large consulting firm, of which executive search is but a division. Or the executive search firm may work in a more restricted area related to executive search, such as executive compensation and personnel functions.

Most executive search firms are off-shoots of management consulting firms, and many of their people formerly worked in this function at such firms. For example, Heidrick and Struggles and Spencer Stuart and Associates were both started by people who formerly worked in executive search at Booz, Allen & Hamilton.

More recently, CPA firms have entered into this activity, and most of the "Big Eight" have established separate organizations to carry on executive search. As mentioned earlier, CPA's have always helped their clients to obtain financial people, and thus embarking on this activity in a formal manner was a natural step.

The highly competitive business climate in the U. S., which continuously searches for improved management talent, plus the overall mobility of executives these days, combine to provide a major market for this type of work. The emergence of large business organizations through acquisitions or mergers has often expanded position responsibilities to the point where they are beyond the capabilities of people in those positions. Executive search became a part of consulting primarily because of the need to staff new positions with capable people. Often these new positions developed out of systems improvement work being done by the consultants. No system will function well without adequate people to direct it. Therefore, personnel improvement is a necessary part of any program of systems improvement.

* * *

This chapter has pointed out the various types of practitioners in the field of management consulting. It has traced their origins and commented on their strengths and weaknesses. This information should permit a general understanding of the profession and the entities that comprise it. With this understanding, it is in order to turn to the market that the profession serves.

The chapter that follows describes briefly the types of clients that the various practitioners of management consulting work with in providing consulting assistance.

6

Clients—An Overview

To the consultant, all the world is his market. To be precise, he regards any entity of a size large enough to warrant his fee as a potential candidate for his services.

Generally, however, the consulting profession looks at the market in terms of three major categories: Industry, Government, and Institutions. In this chapter, I will indicate, for each of these categories, the types of clients that use consultants and the more common types of services provided to each.

Industry

We normally think of three areas, manufacturing, trade, and services, as falling into this category. In the manufacturing area, consultants have done a great deal of work— 49 percent of their total work in 1971, according to a survey made by ACME. This was the first area where significant amounts of work were done. Manufacturing provided the setting for the pioneers of the profession, who instituted basic methods of analysis and time study work. These early efforts, however, have since expanded to include most aspects of manufacturing operations, from long-range planning to records management. A large amount of work is still being done in the area of compensation and management methods, and this is now being supplemented by significant amounts of work dealing with general management, marketing, and finance.

The small-to-medium-size manufacturer has probably produced more work for consultants in relation to his total volume of sales than has any other user of consulting services. Traditionally, the consultant did most of his work for companies with a sales volume ranging from $12,000,-000 to $100,000,000. (This figure, of course, has been revised upward with inflation.) However, with the mergers and acquisitions that occurred during the sixties, many of the small-to-medium-sized manufacturers were acquired by larger companies. Many of these larger companies had their own internal expertise, which they substituted for the services previously provided by consultants. Thus, a significant part of this market has disappeared. The previously mentioned ACME survey shows that the percent of work done in manufacturing declined from 73.7 in 1965 to 49.5 in 1971.

The second area of industry is trade—both wholesale and retail. Retail trade accounts for a larger part of the ultimate sales price of a product than ever before. This is due largely to the increased costs of labor. This increase also occurred in manufacturing, but was offset, at least partially, by the use of labor-saving devices. About the only labor-saving device that is available in trade is to reduce the level of service to the customer.

The increased importance of trade is reflected in the volume of consulting work done in this area. The same ACME study shows that the percent of work done by consultants in the area of wholesale and retail trade increased from 4.0 in 1964 to 7.6 in 1971.

While trade has not offered as many opportunities for consulting as has manufacturing in the past, there are today a number of distinct services that the consultant can provide. One of these is a technique referred to as programmed store staffing. This is a system that predetermines the expected patronage of a store for each hour of the day and each day of the week, and determines the number of clerks needed to provide the desired level of service at all times. This eliminates, to a large extent, a surplus of clerks during the off-peak hours and a shortage during the peak hours. Properly applied. this system has been quite effective in reducing costs without reducing the level of service to customers.

Some other forms of assistance to trade have been: improved forecasting of customer demand as a step toward improved inventory control, improved scheduling and maintenance of vehicles, and better selection of distribution points. Some consultants have also assisted clients in the selection of sites for retail stores. And last but not least has been assistance in the use of data processing in trade. Early applications included accounts receivable and payable, accounting, and inventory control. Today, these applications have been extended to point-of-sale recording systems, where optical scanning devices record the price and stock number of each commodity sold, compute the bill for the customer, and determine the volume of each item sold and the effect on inventory.

The third area of industry is services. This includes banking, insurance, and various types of technical services, such as engineering and legal. In banking, consultants' work increased greatly with the introduction of the computer. Practically all banks now use computers to process checks and keep customer accounts, and the computer has been indispensable in the operation of bank credit card systems. Many of these applications required the assistance of consultants. Another facet of consulting work in banks was the development of systems of mathematically rating the reliability of credit applicants—credit scoring. In credit scoring systems, banks and other lending agencies analyze their past experience to determine what factors distinguish "good" payers from "poor" payers and then use this information to develop benchmarks for distinguishing between them.

Insurance companies have also been great users of EDP equipment. They have used computers not only for developing the statistical information needed for underwriting and reporting, but also for printing premium notices and certain portions of insurance policies, themselves. Some insurance companies have been using credit scoring systems like those employed by banks to help them distinguish between good risks and bad risks. Agency accounting and payroll accounting have been other EDP applications for insurance companies.

In both banks and insurance companies, clerical cost reduction has been important. With the rising level of clerical salary costs, these companies cannot afford to utilize the services of their employees carelessly. In recent years, many consultants have worked at simplifying the procedures followed in offices and determining the volume of work that should be expected from each clerk. Significant reductions in clerical costs have been attained in this manner.

In the other direction, a new area of consulting has emerged in industry. This is the area of job enrichment, which is intended to enlarge the scope of the task performed by an individual employee to the point where it becomes more significant and thus more interesting to him. Successful use of this technique has not only improved production but also, even more importantly, has reduced absenteeism and turnover significantly.

In the technical and professional areas, consultants have assisted in improving accounting and budgeting procedures and systems for allocating profits in accordance with the efforts of principals to produce them. Paperwork simplification and other forms of clerical cost reduction have also been used quite extensively.

Government

The percentage of Gross National Product going to the Government has doubled within the last few years. This is due not only to increased expenditures for national defense but also to new and expanded programs for improving the quality of life of the average and, especially, the disadvantaged citizen. Coincident with this has come a significant increase in salary and wage scales of government employees at all levels. Cities, counties, and school districts are now encountering unionization and accompanying demands for increased salary and fringe benefits and improved working conditions. A recent article in *Business Week* indicated that expenses of cities increased over 100 per cent between 1967 and 1972, and the work of consultants in helping government has more than quadrupled between 1964 and 1971 according to the ACME survey.

Helping to develop and implement new programs in the health, education, and welfare sector has been a major field of endeavor for consultants. And growing out of this has come important work done for local governments and for schools and hospitals. Developing EDP systems to complement these programs also has produced a significant volume of consulting work. Particularly at the local government level, programs have been developed to improve the procurement and control of supplies and provide more effective utilization of employees through work simplification. Vehicle maintenance and scheduling have also been important projects at the state and local level.

One particularly interesting engagement I was involved in for a state government was helping the state auditor install a system of operational auditing that would give him a good look at the operations of the agency and the benefits received from these operations, as well as the manner in which funds were expended and accounted for.

Government is also using consulting to a significant degree because of the desire of government administrators to obtain outside counselling and guidance to reinforce their decisions and thus protect themselves from adverse criticism by political opponents. The rigidity of government pay scales and budgets also produces a need for consultants, not only to provide technical knowhow but also to provide additional manpower when needed quickly and for relatively short periods of time.

Institutions

Institutions, as thought of here, include those involved in education and health care, trade and other associations, and religious organizations.

Educational institutions, until recently, made only limited use of consulting services. Now, however, with the increase in costs of teachers and facilities and a decline in the enrollment of students these institutions have been turning to consultants for assistance, primarily in non-educational areas. Administration, maintenance, feeding and housing, and transportation have been primary areas of work. Consultants have also assisted in eliminating unnecessary courses and in more effectively scheduling the utilization of teachers, and in implementing the use of a single set of facilities by two or more schools, which has helped to reduce costs significantly.

In the field of health care, a great deal has been done by consultants. The amount of work done by consultants in this area nearly doubled between 1964 and 1971. The scheduling of nurses in accordance with patient demand has been very effective in reducing costs. Better control over assessing and collecting charges for laboratory and other extra services has significantly increased hospital income, and overall reviews of financial planning have eliminated unnecessary expansion of facilities and produced more effective budgeting and financial control techniques. In most cases, consultants have assisted in making these improvements.

Associations have not normally been great sources of consulting work. What has been done for them has been largely in the area of data processing, such as developing systems for using the computer for billing and for developing membership rolls and classifying members. One interesting piece of work done for an association was that done for the AICPA. Consultants assisted this Association in developing a data retrieval system covering alternative ways of presenting financial information and permitting the accessing of this data from remote terminals located in the offices of individual firms of CPA's. Presumably, this concept could also be utilized by other trade and industry associations.

Religious organizations, perhaps surprisingly, have been good clients of consultants. One firm did a significant amount of work reviewing the organization and operations of the Southern Baptist Convention, and a CPA firm has done an extensive amount of consulting work in a large archdiocese of the Catholic Church. This included financial and other counselling for the archdiocesan headquarters, and similar guidance to convents and hospitals under the overall direction of the archdiocese.

*   *   *

In this chapter I have attempted to describe the more important types of clients and the types of work done for these clients. This description is by no means intended to be all-inclusive. However, it should give the reader an indication of the ability of consultants to serve almost any large entity, and to indicate the more significant areas of services rendered in each of the three major categories of clients—Industry, Government, and Institutions.

In the next chapter, I shall set forth some guidelines that consultants follow in determining what types of clients to work for and the conditions under which they accept engagements.

7

Selecting Clients

Many articles have been written telling clients how to select consultants, but little, if anything, has been written to tell consultants how to select clients. Selecting clients is extremely important to the professional success of the consultant, because consulting is a two-way relationship. The consultant and the client must work together with mutual understanding and respect.

Requirements for a Successful Engagement

In order for an engagement to be successful, several factors must be operative in the arrangement. The first of these is the recognition by the client that a problem exists or is likely to exist. One might ask why, if the client did not believe that a problem existed, he would engage a consultant in the first place. The answer is that sometimes a client wants to use the consultant as a rubber stamp and therefore is not prone to recognize weaknesses that the consultant points out to him.

A second factor needed for successful consulting work is a sincere desire on the part of the client to take whatever steps are necessary to correct the weaknesses identified. Sometimes clients will pay lip service to this concept without having a deep conviction that they must make the changes necessary to rectify the shortcomings that the consultant detects. These clients would like to see conditions improved, but they are unwilling to take the necessary steps. This frequently occurs with top executives who are weak and unwilling to make needed organizational and procedural changes because they are unsure of their ability to successfully deal with the problems that must be overcome in making these changes.

The third factor is a willingness on the part of management to make disclosure of vital information to the consultant. Some clients like to play games with the consultant. They like to see what he can find out unassisted. This is like going to a doctor and not telling him what symptoms you have. He may be able to find out without your assistance, but he can do so more quickly and more accurately with your assistance. The ideal client situation in this regard is one wherein top management discloses all pertinent information helpful to the consultant and requests that all other people in the organization do the same. Many consultants request a letter from the president to this effect as the first step in beginning an engagement. This information can take many forms. It can be information provided in interviews, or statistics and reports from both within and without the company. It can even include comments regarding the activities of competitors and reasons why the client is not taking similar actions.

A fourth factor is the willingness of the client to assist the consultant. While consultants can work without client assistance, they cannot be truly effective in such circumstances. The kind of assistance that the consultant should get from the client includes:

1. Defining problems
2. Gathering information
3. Evaluating alternative solutions to problems
4. Suggesting modifications of recommendations as needed
5. Disclosing, promptly, any doubts and problems encountered by the client concerning the conduct of the engagement
6. Implementing recommendations.

Most of these are self-explanatory; however, the last two need some comment.

When a dentist works on your teeth and through an improper procedure proceeds to cause pain unnecessarily, you of course tell him so, so that he can correct his procedure. However, many clients when they see the consultant omitting an apparently important area of information, will not mention this omission to him. Or, in some cases, the consultants on the job may be irritating client people and are not quickly told about it. Or the consultants' efforts in certain areas may appear fruitless to the client. In such cases, a full and frank exchange of views is likely to be of great value to everyone. Usually, any engagement conducted without the active participation of the client will not only cost more but will also be less productive.

I would also like to comment here, about the importance of the client's assisting the consultant in implementing recommendations, for this produces a number of benefits. It helps to ensure that the consultant will take into consideration all pertinent factors in installing his recommendations. It provides for training the people who will operate the new systems, and these people will then have the opportunity to understand the concepts upon which the recommendations were based and will be better able to know when to modify these recommendations as conditions change in the future. And finally, it should significantly reduce the consultant's· fees.

A fifth factor necessary for a successful engagement is the willingness of the client to pay for services rendered. This hardly needs mentioning, except in situations where it is difficult for the consultant to be precise in estimating his fees in advance of the engagement. After the initial review, the consultant will sometimes believe that the scope or extent of the engagement should be changed, and this may affect his fee. The client who is unwilling to recognize the need to permit a justly arrived at change in the fee is not a satisfactory client. The matter of fees is discussed in some detail in a later chapter; however, it is pertinent at this point to comment that a lack of mutual confidence between the client and the consultant, such that it will prevent the client paying the rightfully earned fee of the consultant, is certainly a serious impediment to a successful engagement.

A sixth factor is compatibility between the client and the consulting team. People are people, and no two clients are alike nor are any two consultants who serve them. Properly matching personalities of the top client people and the consulting people is an important requirement for engagement success. Large firms of consultants probably have an advantage in this respect, since they have a larger staff to choose from in matching their people with those of the client. It is usually easier to change people on the consulting team than to ask the client to provide other people to work on the project.

The presence of these six factors in a client engagement will not automatically assure the success of an engagement, but the lack of any one of them can certainly imperil it. Therefore, any client who will not make a determined effort to provide an environment in which these elements exist is not a satisfactory client, and the consultant who works with such a client will incur a high risk of failure.

Potential Danger Signals

The consultant needs to be aware of certain conditions that signal potential danger in accepting a consulting engagement. The first of these is when the client seems to already know what he wants the consultant to say. There is nothing wrong with an executive who has strong convictions, and most executives have in the back of their minds a deep feeling of what the consultant may find in their organizations and may recommend. However, what the consultant should guard against is the client who wants to use the consultant as a rubber stamp for his own point of view. If the consultant truly believes that the client will not objectively accept his findings and consider his recommendations, he would be better off refusing to accept the engagement.

The second is when a client indicates early in the engagement that he does not want to change anything and wants the consultant to support his efforts to maintain the *status quo*. In such situations, client executives, recognizing the desires of their Boards of Directors or other influential people to make changes in company operations, will want to use consultants as an excuse for not making the changes requested. They will do this in a number of ways. They will attempt to convince the consultant that they are right in the face of evidence to the contrary, or they will use the consultant as a delaying tactic. In such cases, the client, rather than making required changes, calls in a consulting firm to "look at the situation and then make recommendations," knowing full well that any recommendations of the consultant that disagree with the client's wishes will be disputed and disregarded. Another tactic is to use the consultant to confuse the issue. If the consultant presents one point of view and the client another, third parties will be left uncertain as to the true situation, and the issue will remain clouded and the necessary corrective action will not be taken.

A third potential danger signal exists when a consultant is to be used to settle a fight in the organization. The objectivity of the consultant can be used very effectively in a situation where there is an honest difference of opinion. However, when the situation gets beyond that point, and one or another of the warring factions has become so deeply entrenched that graceful acceptance of the consultant's recommendation is impossible, a consultant must recognize that either one or the other of these factions is going to look upon him as one of the enemy, and his attempts to help will end in futility.

A fourth potential danger signal arises when the client does not appear to be willing to make the changes needed. The consultant will do his best to develop worthwhile recommendations, and these are put into a report. However, the client will let the report lie on the shelf without ever taking action. This, of course, is a waste of the client's money and of the consultant's efforts. This is not to imply that the client must always act on the consultant's recommendations, but he should refrain from doing so only in cases where the consultant's recommendations are clearly unsound or are impracticable at the time. A free interchange of information between client and consultant goes a long way towards eliminating the possibility of unsound or impracticable recommendations by the consultant.

A fifth potential danger signal is an indication that the client may not be in a position to make the changes needed. In the case of government, certain laws and regulations may prohibit making the changes needed and it may not be possible at the time of the engagement, or within a reasonable time, to obtain changes in these laws to permit implementing the consultant's recommendations. In the case of a business or institutional entity, the client may not have the resources needed to implement the recommendations. The company may be in a line of business that is rapidly disappearing, and may not have the capability to change to another line of business. A consultant, recognizing these conditions, would be ill-advised to take on an engagement for that client.

A sixth potential danger signal is an expectation on the part of the client that the consultant will do the work entirely without assistance from the client. This has been previously commented upon and needs no further explanation here.

A seventh danger signal emerges when the client expects results in too short a time. Results cannot be produced overnight, and, regardless of the size of the team that a consultant will put on the job, in every situation there is a certain minimum amount of time necessary to gain the facts needed and to develop sound and meaningful recommendations. There is also an additional minimum time needed to implement these recommendations. Consultants must recognize the fact that some clients have a tendency to put off asking for assistance, and once having made the decision to do so, expect the engagement to be started at once and completed almost immediately. While it is usually possible to convince a client that it takes a reasonable amount of time to get the results of a consulting engagement, once in a while a client is encountered who will not permit adequate time. In such cases, the consultant would be wise to decline the engagement.

An eighth danger signal is when the client unduly restricts the scope of the study. This can occur in several ways. The client may, for example, ask the consultant to develop an inventory control system without permitting him to inquire into the manner in which sales forecasts are developed. Or the client may want the consultant to work at too low a level—to develop a cost accounting system without consulting the controller or the production superintendent, or to do the job without the consent or knowledge of top management. In all these situations, the consultant is not likely to get the information and organizational support needed to develop or carry out recommendations effectively.

A ninth potential danger signal manifests itself when the client is unwilling to pay a realistic fee. Here the client will insist that the work be done for no more than a given amount, and he expects the consultant to reduce either his efforts or his profit to the point where he can do the job for this fee. This is indicative of a client who is likely to prevent the consultant from being truly effective, even if the consultant is willing to do all the work that is necessary on the engagement regardless of the profitability of the job. If the client does not regard the engagement as sufficiently important to justify a reasonable fee, it is quite likely that the client will not properly respect the work done and properly support the implementation of recommended changes. This is not to say that the consultant should have an unlimited scope of operation or that the client or the consultant should not suggest ways in which the work on the engagement can be reduced so as to permit carrying out the engagement at a more modest fee. I remember one instance when we obtained an engagement at least partly through our conviction that a survey of only four manufacturing plants out of seventeen (provided these four plants were carefully selected) would produce results representative of those existing in all the plants. This turned out to be the case. The danger signal that the consultant should be aware of is not the client's legitimate desire to reduce the cost of the study but his failure to properly recognize the importance of the study itself.

Unfortunately, inexperienced consultants may either not be aware of these potential danger signals or may tend to ignore them in their desire to get business, believing that these obstacles can somehow be overcome in the course of the engagement. Occasionally this can occur— but the odds are against it. And when consultants have done work under these conditions, they have usually produced work of so poor a quality that it has tended to erode the confidence of the general public in the consulting profession. Experienced consulting firms have learned these lessons and will usually turn down clients whom they consider unsatisfactory.

* * *

Having indicated the nature of consulting work and the firms that engage in such work, and the types of clients and situations that limit the chances of a successful engagement, I shall next indicate, from an insider's point of view, how to select a consultant.

8

Finding the
Right Consultant

The subject of selecting a consultant has already been dealt with in several excellent articles, as I have mentioned before. For the most part, these articles have been written by people who have used consultants or who represent the viewpoint of those who have used them. However, I believe that it might be well to have the viewpoint of one who is in the profession. To the best of my knowledge, no one in the profession has written on this subject, except in proposals or brochures that are designed to show a client that a particular consultant or consulting firm is well qualified to do consulting work in some particular area.

As mentioned in Chapter 1, it is almost impossible for an individual or company to be objective in self-appraisal, and I doubt that I can be completely objective in writing on this subject, no matter how hard I try. Therefore, in evaluating my comments, the reader will have to allow for any built-in prejudices that might unintentionally manifest themselves. On the other hand, it might be of special interest to get the point of view of someone who has observed, from the inside, the impact of the various factors responsible for the success or failure of a large number of engagements.

But again, in taking up this subject, I would caution the reader that because of the wide variety of sizes and types of engagements it is very difficult to generalize on the factors relevant to the selection of a consultant. A large, complex engagement, for example, requires careful attention to a number of factors in choosing a consultant, whereas a small and simple engagement might require less detailed appraisal of the consultant's suitability.

In general, however, five factors should be considered in selecting a consultant:

1. Integrity
2. Responsibility
3. Capability
4. Cost
5. Personality.

The significance of each of these factors is discussed below.

Integrity

Integrity may not always be considered as carefully as capability, but in buying any product, it is my belief that one should never willingly deal with a person or firm of whom one cannot be absolutely sure—particularly when buying an intangible commodity like consulting advice. With the proper contractual and surety safeguards, it may be possible to do business with just about anyone, but the uncertainties that surround such a difficult-to-define thing as a consulting engagement strongly favor dealing with a person or firm who can always be trusted to do the right thing—in other words, one whose integrity is absolute. Unfortunately, there is a certain amount of evidence of the need to check out the integrity of a consulting firm that is being seriously considered for an engagement.

By integrity I mean honesty and straightforwardness in describing the firm's capabilities and in promising what can be accomplished, and at what cost. Integrity also includes the manifestation of a genuine desire to produce results, and the possession of personal and professional scruples against practices that are dubious or questionable.

The best indicator of a consulting firm's integrity comes from having used the firm before. Usually, any weaknesses will become apparent in the performance of one or more engagements for a client, although sometimes a firm will perform well on a small first engagement and less well on a larger follow-up engagement.

Recommendations of others who have used the firm are also good indicators of integrity. Here, again, a word of caution. It is best to get recommendations from someone personally known to you or to people you trust. Bankers, lawyers, and CPA's are good people to use in checking on the integrity of consultants. Their connections are usually widespread enough to bring to light any instances of substandard behavior on the part of a consultant.

Responsibility

A consulting firm may wish to perform responsibly on an engagement but may not have the capability to do so. I am not referring here to technical capability (which is discussed below), but to financial, personnel, and physical resources. The firm may have on its staff consultants who are well qualified technically, but it may not have sufficient money, people, or other facilities to perform successfully. The money needed to even start an engagement may not be available, or the money needed for travel, or to obtain statistical or other services necessary for the engagement—even though progress payments are received as the work proceeds. The firm may not have the staff needed to do the work, or somebody to carry on if the consultant assigned to the engagement becomes sick or disabled. Or it may not have sufficient staff to do follow-up work if needed.

If a client has not used a consulting firm before, he may wish to get a financial statement or a Dun and Bradstreet report before engaging that firm. And, of course, obtaining references from other clients, where possible, is always good practice.

Capability

Apart from integrity and responsibility, the capability of the consultant or consultants assigned to the engagement to effectively carry out the work is the most important requirement. This capability has a number of facets.

The first is intelligence. The consultant must be able to learn and learn fast—not only what the client wants, but also what the client really needs (if the two are not synonymous, and they often aren't), the inner workings of the client company, and the impact that needed changes might have on that company. In addition, the consultant needs to be imaginative and creative, so that he can develop recommendations ideally suited to the client rather than the same tried and true methods that every other client uses.

Training, too, is important—particularly in the specialized technical areas that are to be dealt with in the engagement. If it is a marketing study, it is essential to have a consultant trained in marketing; if it is a manufacturing study, it is essential to have a consultant trained in industrial engineering. Also, a consultant has to be trained in obtaining facts and in analyzing them and developing solutions to problems encountered. Fact-finding, to be done well, requires training in dealing with and understanding people; the consultant must learn to evaluate not only what people tell him but also, in some cases, why they tell him. Finally, the consultant must be trained to communicate, both orally and in writing. Training in liberal arts and in the social sciences is especially applicable to these last-mentioned aspects of consulting work.

Another important attribute is experience—both the experience of the firm and the experience of the people who work on the engagement. And there *is* a difference. Many firms can point to a great deal of applicable experience, but, because of the rapid turnover of consultants, the firm may no longer have with it the people who did the work. On large engagements, many clients will ask for résumés of the men who will work on the engagements, so as to have a good idea of their training and experience. Often this becomes a critical point in the selection of one consulting firm over another.

But a word of warning in this respect. Many clients insist on having a consultant with experience in the same type of work and in the same industry. This *can* be a mistake. If the job is the same, and the industry is the same, there may be a tendency on the part of the consultant to believe that the problems and their solutions are the same. There is a real danger that the client will only be brought up to the standards of the industry.

And this is really not enough—the consultant should provide the client with something beyond a textbook or run-of-mill solution to his problem.

Some of the more significant breakthroughs I have known have occurred when intelligent, creative consultants, working in an industry unfamiliar to them, came up with ideas novel to the industry. In one case, a consulting firm inexperienced in sugar plantations came up with a new method of valuing growing sugar cane, with a consequent reduction in income tax of about $1,000,000. In another case, a consultant used, in a machine tool company, a system of inventory pricing that was being used by the U. S. Veterans Administration to price its inventory of pharmaceuticals. And in this latter case, the consultant recommended an actual cost system instead of the traditional standard cost system, because the number of component parts was high and their annual usage was low.

However, while experience in the same industry is not always beneficial, previous experience with the client is a definite advantage. If the consultant already knows a great deal about the client's operations and organization, he need not spend time learning these things during an engagement. Also, he will require less of the client's time in carrying out the work.

An experienced consultant will often perceive that the client's problem may be other than what the client thinks. Inadequate sales forecasts as a cause of inventory shortages, poor organization as a cause of personnel turnover, or inadequate R&D or, perhaps, intense price competition, as a cause of declining sales are examples of underlying defects often overlooked by clients. I remember an instance where a brewery client wanted a paperwork study. The consultant asked for a tour of the brewery, and, in making that tour, discovered an abnormally fast bottling line that had a significant spillage loss because of faulty maintenance of the bottling equipment. By assisting the client to correct this problem, the consultant reduced the client's costs much more than he did by simplifying the client's paperwork—which he also did, with good results.

The best measure of the capability of a consultant is the thoroughness of his understanding of the client's problem and the soundness of his approach toward solving it. This is the hallmark of a true professional. This is where experience counts.

Cost

I have purposely relegated cost to fourth place, not because I don't think it is important, but because I think it is less important than other factors in the selection of a consultant. Some potential users of consultants would like to buy these services in the same way that they would buy a commodity—the lowest price that meets the specifications. Unfortunately for them, consultants' services cannot be measured with the precision of commodities or other material items. Therefore, price should not be the only consideration in selecting a consultant, any more than it should be in selecting a lawyer or a doctor.

At one time, this problem became particularly acute in dealing with government units where there was a long tradition of requesting bids (or proposals) from all potentially qualified consultants and awarding contracts to the lowest bidder. Some reputable consultants therefore refused to submit proposals on government work. Now, however, most of the more progressive units of government use price as only one factor in selecting a consultant. I remember an instance where a state asked for proposals and received fee quotations ranging from $27,000 to $150,000. They very wisely rejected the $27,000 proposer, as one who did not understand what the state required. They elected, instead, a firm that understood the problem and was well qualified to do the work—at a fee of $120,000.

In consulting, as with most things, you get what you pay for. And the fee proposals of experienced and qualified consultants will often be surprisingly close—without, of course, there being collusion among them. The reason is that, particularly with a well worded request for proposal, each firm will see about the same amount of work to be done, and each firm will have about the same salary, overhead, and profit objectives, and will thus have similar fee quotations.

Nevertheless, it is not necessary to accept without question the fee quoted by a consultant. There are several measures that can be used to evaluate fees. The first is the amount of time the consultant requires to do the job. Is it reasonable in the light of work to be done? Does it appear to provide for only the amount of fact-finding that seems to be necessary? Similarly, are the amounts of time spent for analysis, implementation, and report writing adequate? Does the staffing appear to be reasonable?

A second measure is the hourly billing rates to be used. Are they reasonable, considering the expertise and experience of the people to be assigned to the engagement?

A key question the client should ask himself is "Are the fees compatible with the benefits expected?" If not, the work should not be undertaken. If they are, the assurance of quality work is more important than getting the work done for the lowest possible price. A man facing trial on a serious charge does not shop for an attorney on the basis of price alone.

A final point to bear in mind is that a consulting firm that has, or expects to have, a continuing relationship with a client will normally charge only a reasonable fee for its services.

Personality

The personality of a consultant is like frosting on a cake. It can enhance a good product but it cannot save a bad one. Nevertheless, if you have a choice between two well qualified consultants, it is only natural to pick the one whose personality or style of operations seems to best fit yours. A good match of personalities between client and consultant is bound to improve the results obtained. I believe that this meshing of personalities in selecting consultants is far more important than most people realize, and deserves more attention than it has received in the past.

As I have already noted in Chapter 7, however, a consulting engagement is a two-way relationship, and personality conflicts or disagreements concerning the consultant's investigative techniques or interpretation of facts as the job proceeds can still cause incompatibilities in this relationship.

In any case, a consultant's sensitivity to people is a key indicator of his ability. A man who listens attentively to what people tell him, will not only get the information he needs, but will also get the cooperation needed to use that information in implementing the changes needed to solve the client's problem.

A client can also judge a consultant on the basis of the speeches he has given and the articles he has written. These can be good indicators of a consultant's understanding of the factors that govern his ability to develop solutions to remedy the problems clients face. However, the client should be aware that the consultant's ability to think about and write about a problem does not in itself indicate the ability to effectively organize and carry out a large-scale consulting effort. The two skills don't always go together.

* * *

All too often a glib tongue promising unattainable results, the blind acceptance of recommendations of colleagues, or a low price has been the basis for selecting consultants. The results have not been good for the clients or for the consulting profession in such cases. Careful attention to the five factors dealt with in this chapter should help clients to make better selections of consultants.

In the next chapter, I shall attempt to give some insight into how, once the client and the consultant have selected each other, the actual work of a consulting engagement is carried on.

9

How the Practice Is Carried On

This chapter deals with what I regard as the basic types of consulting work. It excludes executive search, which, although it is considered a form of consulting by some practitioners and is therefore offered as a service by some consultants, is significantly different from other types of consulting work. Executive search is dealt with in the next chapter.

There are an endless number of variations in the ways that consulting work is carried on. These variations largely reflect the types of practitioners and the types of engagements being dealt with. The overview presented in this book cannot, of course, encompass all the myriad variations in consulting practice, and therefore I have confined my remarks to what I believe generally constitutes common practice in project-type consulting work carried out by independent consultants. Project-type consulting, as used here, refers to engagements where a specific project is worked on for a specific period of time and is identified in these terms. It differs from the retainer type of arrangement, where consultants give advice over periods of time on an as-required basis.

In this chapter I indicate what I believe to be generally followed practice in the following areas:

Developing the practice
Securing the engagement
Organizing the engagement
Carrying out the engagement
Billing the engagement
Following up on the engagement.

Each of these areas is described in some detail below.

Developing the Practice

Practice development is extremely important to the average consultant. Unlike an auditor, where the client needs him every year, or an attorney, where a continuing succession of legal problems and general corporate work require continuous guidance, the consultant usually performs a series of unrelated engagements and each of these engagements has to be developed independently. In addition, most clients will not need consultants all the time nor will they always want to use the same consultants, because of the vastly differing skills required to solve different problems. Therefore, the consultant must continuously contact existing clients and potential new clients.

The manner in which clients can be contacted is governed by ethical, and sometimes legal, restraints. Each of the organizations to which consulting firms belong has its own set of rules governing contacts with potential clients. Both ACME and IMC, for example, do not prohibit direct solicitation of clients, but both do prohibit a member consultant from working for a client in the same area in which another consultant is working. And both ACME and IMC allow advertising as long as it is in good taste. On the other hand, AICPA, to which most CPA consultants belong, does prohibit direct solicitation of clients and requires firms doing consulting work for clients audited by another CPA to notify that CPA before beginning work for the client. In addition, laws of State Boards of Accountancy have, in some cases, prohibited quoting fees competitively.

These restrictions require that consultants gain clients in a less direct fashion. A prime form of practice development, therefore, is through personal contacts. A consultant who does not have the time, inclination, or ability to meet potential clients will have a great deal of difficulty in gaining engagements unless his work is so outstanding that it causes clients to seek him out. As a result, many principals in consulting firms belong to organizations where they are apt to meet potential clients. Chambers of Commerce, service clubs, community fund drives, luncheon clubs, and golf clubs are examples of such organizations. The principals of some consulting firms make a point of living in areas where potential client executives may reside, so that they will meet them at the railroad station, or, socially, through church and school activities.

Some firms also make a point of establishing personal contacts within all large potential client organizations. One consulting firm in particular has made extensive use of this technique; each employee, when he joins the firm, has to file a list of his acquaintances who might be influential at some future time in assisting the firm in getting business. These lists are supplemented by lists of people who leave the consulting firm to take positions in outside organizations. These lists are kept up-to-date, and are used to identify helpful contacts when the firm is trying to do business with any of these organizations. The degree of effort that this firm continues to put into this practice indicates it has been quite successful in obtaining work through these contacts.

Obtaining recommendations from satisfied clients is an important form of practice development. Any potential client, before engaging a consultant with whom he has not worked before, should, and usually does, check with a former client of that consultant. Thus, all good consultants are very aware of the importance of each engagement, and strive to provide their clients with creative solutions, good graphics, and well written reports. Businessmen generally like to talk about what they have been doing, and if they have been using consultants and this is generally known or is not to be kept secret, these businessmen are usually eager to tell their colleagues or associates what a good job the consultant has done. Bankers, attorneys, and CPA's are often good sources of recommendations for consultants. (If the CPA believes that he can do a good consulting job for a client, he will say so; otherwise, he will recommend another firm.) In addition, consultants themselves will usually have a list of clients whom they are sure will give them good recommendations.

Most management consulting firms will use promotional materials as a form of practice development. These materials may be merely a list of the offices of the firm and the areas in which it practices. Or they may contain some thought-provoking comments about a matter of importance at the moment, or surveys of particular aspects of today's business conditions. They may, for instance, summarize what a number of prominent companies have done to meet certain problems, such as cost reduction or new product development. Promotions and personnel changes within consulting firms are also usually reported on the financial pages of local newspapers.

CPA firms, on the other hand, are prohibited from making use of many of these promotional vehicles because of ethical restrictions of the AICPA. CPA firms are forbidden to send out general mailings of promotional material, and sending materials other than to the audit clients of the firm can be done only upon request. A good example of how stringently this restriction is enforced occurred recently when one large international CPA firm achieved a great deal of publicity by issuing to its employees financial data regarding the operation of the firm. This information, of course, found its way into the hands of editors of financial journals and was immediately commented upon in these journals, primarily because it was the first financial information of this type that had been published by any CPA firm. The AICPA received numerous complaints from other CPA firms disapproving of this publicity.

Many consulting firms make extensive use of publications and lectures. They welcome the opportunity to have qualified members of their staff speak before groups that may contain top executives of potential clients, and some firms have made a point of doing research in certain areas and then publishing material summarizing the results obtained. One partner in a CPA firm recently published a book whose main theme was the need for the government to use business management principles in guiding its operations. Many consultants contribute to handbooks dealing with various management disciplines, and some have written books on certain specialized fields, such as industrial, engineering, marketing, and finance. Altogether, writing and lecturing are important parts of practice development.

Consulting firms belonging to ACME and consultants belonging to IMC are allowed to advertise, if it is done in good taste. CPA firms, on the other hand, are not allowed to advertise in any manner. Boldface listings or multiple listings in a phone directory are forbidden, as is listing the CPA firm as a contributor to charity. Some of the consulting firms that belong to no association restricting the quality of advertising have gone all out. For example, one firm holding itself out as a consultant had, for years, its name on a lighted sign overlooking Union Square in San Francisco. Needless to say, however, most consultants adhere to the principle that, in marketing services to a rather sophisticated group of buyers, advertising must be done in good taste if it is to attract the type of client that a reputable consulting firm would like to have.

Direct solicitation of clients *must* be avoided by all CPA firms and is generally avoided by many consulting firms. But, here again, some relatively large consulting firms have resorted to direct solicitation in order to obtain new business. They have developed and capitalized on specific techniques, such as cost reduction, and have directly solicited business from companies whom they thought might become clients. I know of one consultant in a large ACME firm who, recognizing the potential in a particular manufacturer, used all possible contacts to get introduced to the client. When it became apparent that this was not immediately possible, and with time running out, he finally made a cold canvass call on the client to get an engagement, and was successful.

Thus it can be seen that consulting firms have at their disposal a number of means to practice development, and they use them to the extent that their particular position in the profession permits.

Securing the Engagement

Consultants usually secure engagements by making proposals for such work to the client. Such proposals may be either solicited or unsolicited. Solicited proposals usually evolve from one of the practice development activities described above.

Practice development, however, is only a means of obtaining a potential client's interest in having the consultant work for him. This interest can be expressed in several ways. It can be merely a request that an individual consultant come in and discuss a particular problem that the client has in mind, or the client may choose to speak to several firms regarding his problem. In private industry, a consultant is usually able to meet face-to-face with the potential client in advance and, in effect, interest him to the point where he will ask the consultant to submit a proposal.

In other cases, such as government engagements, the client may prepare an elaborate request for proposal, from which he expects to obtain proposals from all consultants who might be interested. Often a public meeting will be scheduled for all interested consultants. At this meeting the request for proposal is reviewed and questions of consultants are answered. Sometimes such a meeting will result in a revision of the request for proposal if it is ambiguous or incomplete. Consultants are very coy at such meetings. They attempt to find out who else is there, so that they have some idea of who their competition is. Also, they will be very careful regarding the questions they ask, to be sure that they do not indicate to their competitors any original ideas they might have concerning how the engagement might be carried out.

Unsolicited proposals are often submitted by consultants who believe that they can offer the client a service whose value the client is not fully aware of and, thus, has not requested. This occurs frequently in the case of government agencies.

Responding to a request for a proposal for an engagement in the class where the fee may be half a million dollars or more is usually very expensive. Therefore, many consulting firms will not respond to a request unless they believe that they have a reasonable chance (perhaps one in ten) of getting the work. Thus, in order to be sure to attract the interest of the best qualified consultants, some clients will use a pre-screening process. In this process a client will ask those consultants whom they feel are qualified to do the work to submit their qualifications. Having reviewed these qualifications the client will then submit an invitation to those three, five, or possible ten, firms that the client believes are best qualified to submit a proposal.

Sometimes the request for proposal will indicate the client's willingness to permit interested consultants to visit his premises and work with people knowledgeable in the area to be covered by the study. Most consulting firms will not normally submit a proposal unless a representative is able to do this, because it enables them to structure the proposed engagement in such a way as to be most responsive to the needs of the client. The example cited in a previous chapter, where we proposed to study only four plants instead of seventeen, came out of one of these pre-proposal conferences.

A well defined request for proposals will usually give the basic information that the consultant needs to prepare a proposal. The request will specify the nature of the problem, the scope and nature of the study expected, its location and timing, and sometimes the amount of money available to pay for the study. It will also include a due date for the proposal, dates for the beginning and end of the study, and the nature of the report or other end product desired. The basic contents of a proposal are usually as follows:

Scope of work
Methodology to be employed
Qualifications of the consultant
Time and cost required
Benefits to be received.

Part of this information can be developed from the request for proposal.

The scope of work section of the proposal often includes a definition of the consultant's understanding of the client's objectives, in order to assure that there is a mutual understanding of these objectives between the client and the consultant, and to serve as a sound basis for the scope of the study and the methods to be employed. Consultants will usually spend a considerable amount of time in developing the scope of the study.

They will also devote a great deal of time and effort to detailing the methodology to be used. In effect, they will develop a model of the engagement. Not only does this permit them to be more explicit in their proposal, but it also serves as a good basis for determining skill and staff requirements and the resulting time and fees necessary to do the work.

The section on the firm's qualifications is often referred to as boiler plate. It is usually a description of the firm's background, capabilities, and achievements, and is fairly standard from one proposal to another, usually with only minor changes to emphasize the firm's capabilities that are particularly pertinent to the job at hand. Biographical data on the key people who will work on the engagement are often included in these qualifications, or as a separate section of the proposal. These biographical data include information about education, employment, and related consulting experience. Most consulting firms cannot always be certain that their work schedules will permit using all or only those people whose biographical data have been submitted. Therefore, they reserve the right to substitute other members of their staff having similar qualifications, if this becomes necessary.

Usually, the consultant will specify when he will be able to begin the engagement and how much elapsed time will be needed to complete it. Depending upon the requirements, he will submit a table of man-hours to be worked, broken down by level of skill. The cost of the engagement can be stated in several ways. It can be a lump-sum cost covering time and expenses, or it can be a lump-sum cost for time, plus actual expenses incurred for travel and subsistence of the consultant, and sometimes for report preparation and the use of a computer or other special devices. Sometimes the costs can be an estimate (based upon expected time to be spent extended at standard billing rates), with a limit on the maximum fee to be charged. And sometimes the fee will be actual cost and expense based on an estimate of time and fee, with the understanding that any significant increase over the estimated fee will be cleared in advance with the client. The most flexible of all arrangements is for the consultant to charge standard billing rates and actual expenses. This usually occurs when it is extremely difficult to define the scope of the engagement and the amount of work to be done and when the client has a great deal of confidence in the integrity of the consultant, or when he is the only qualified consultant available and this is the basis upon which he wishes to work.

The proposal letter should serve as the overall statement of what benefits the client wishes to receive, and what steps the consultant will take to provide them. It serves as a contract with the client in cases where the client does not insist on a formal contract. The vast majority of work done for industry and smaller units of government is of this type. A careful review of the proposal letter (or contract) will indicate what the end product of the job will be and how the consultant proposes to produce this end product.

When all proposals have been received, the job of selecting the consultant begins. Again, this process may vary considerably, depending upon the client and the size of the engagement. In many cases, when only one consultant has submitted a proposal, the decision is primarily one of, "Do we want the work and are willing to pay the price?" In other cases, where proposals may have been submitted by two or three firms, the man in charge of obtaining the study, aided by one or two assistants, will evaluate the proposals and first determine which consultants seem to have the best understanding of the problems and the best methods for dealing with them, and then will consider the fee proposed by each. Final selection, then, becomes a process of balancing apparent capabilities with fee to be charged. As I have already mentioned, most sophisticated industrial companies realize that, in the long run, they will get what they pay for, and, therefore will not necessarily choose the consultant whose fee is lowest. On the other hand, if the client has given a good description of the work to be done to two or more well qualified and competent consultants, very often there will not be much difference in the fees quoted.

In studies made for the government, where the fee is often hundreds of thousands of dollars, there is usually a committee to evaluate the proposals. Often, these proposals are submitted in two parts: one containing price, and the other the balance of the information requested. The selection committee will first review the proposals, without the price information being made available to them. They will then rank the proposals in numerical order. The next step is to rank the proposals in terms of price and then correlate the two ranks. Most consultants would like to watch this selection process at work, but unfortunately the only way that they can participate in it is to be part of a selection committee to judge proposals submitted by people other than themselves.

Once the selection is made, the results are communicated to the proposers, usually by mail to the losers and by telephone, followed up by letter, to the winner. Normally, the decisions of the selection committee are accepted without contest, although occasionally in a large engagement, particularly one having political overtones, one or more losing consultants will contest the decision, usually without significant results.

Organizing the Engagement

Properly organizing the engagement is, of course, a key element in its success. It focuses attention on the important steps to be taken, sequences these steps, and provides an effective basis for planning and controlling the work. Organizing the engagement usually requires the following seven steps:

1. Review the proposal to determine the client's objectives and the steps promised to achieve them;
2. Determine the nature of the report or other end product of the engagement;
3. Identify the tasks to be performed to develop the information needed in the report;

4. Determine the sequence in which the various tasks ideally should be performed;
5. Provide review points to determine potential changes in the scope or nature of the work;
6. Select the staff to be used;
7. Cost out the approach developed and modify it if necessary.

Each of these steps is discussed below.

Much of the work of organizing an engagement will already have been done if a comprehensive proposal has been developed. This would have been necessary in order to intelligently quote the time and fee required for the engagement. Moreover, the report or system to be developed constitutes the consultant's product to be produced, and this, in itself, is determined largely on the basis of the proposal letter. A report or system that does not correspond to the client's objectives and the steps whereby the consultant intends to achieve these objectives, as outlined in the proposal, is apt to be grossly deficient.

Some consultants will begin an engagement without a clear understanding of what the end product of that engagement will be. They proceed according to their normal practice and trust that these activities will somehow produce the information necessary to go into the report or system to be developed. This is putting the cart before the horse. An experienced consultant will first review his proposal and then develop an outline of the report or system to be produced. This outline, of course, will be tentative—to be reduced or expanded, depending upon the nature of the information developed, and modified in line with any modifications made in the scope or objective of the engagement. One of the reasons that consultants tend to ignore this step is that it is difficult, because it requires inductive reasoning. It is necessary to determine the nature of the conclusions to be arrived at, the information needed to develop these conclusions, and the logical sources of this information.

This outline can then be used to identify the specific tasks to be performed; for example, interviewing, analyzing data, and charting the flow of information. In cataloguing these tasks it is necessary to bear in mind their importance in the engagement as a whole, and the time and effort that will be needed to carry them out. Once this is done, it is possible to determine the size and the make-up of the staff needed for each task and for the job in total.

With the tasks to be performed clearly identified, they should be sequenced, to determine the order in which each should be taken. For example, the consultant should normally attempt to interview the chief industrial engineer before interviewing the methods analyst. Unfortunately, consultants do not normally have complete liberty in sequencing the tasks to be performed. They must take into consideration the scheduling of the client people. If the advertising manager is leaving on a trip to Europe, it is well to interview him first, even ahead of the vice-president of marketing, if necessary. In addition, the consultant must be flexible to account for unexpected absences of the client people and their inability to meet scheduled appointments.

Providing for review points within the engagement is important. All engagements start out based upon certain premises—explicit or implicit. After the work has gone on for a week or two, the consultant begins to get enough input to determine the relative validity of the basic assumptions made when planning the engagement. To the extent that these assumptions prove invalid, it may be necessary to change the direction, scope, or depth of the work. For example, if it is believed originally that marketing is grossly deficient and that a careful analysis will be needed to provide detailed recommendations for its improvement, and subsequent study discloses that marketing is well run but weaknesses exist in other parts of the sales effort, these findings will be highlighted and dealt with at the review points. These review points should normally include some form of communication with the client, either to assure him that all is going as planned or to discuss with him the need to change the engagement in some manner.

The next step is to determine the staff requirements for the engagement. This, too, will have been done, to a large degree, as part of preparing a comprehensive proposal. The general make-up and specialties of the required staff will have been determined, along with fairly general ideas of the staff time required at each level. At this point, however, it is necessary to be more specific. It is necessary to identify, if possible, the men who will work on the engagement, their billing rates, and how much time will be required of each. Their availability should be determined and communicated to the manpower scheduling group as soon as possible.

When all of these steps have been taken, it will then be possible to cost out the engagement. This figure should be compared with that in the proposal. If it is substantially above the figure quoted in the proposal, the entire scope of the engagement as planned should be reviewed to determine if it is in line with that intended when the proposal was written. If it develops that it is necessary to spend this higher amount in order to do a satisfactory job, this mattter must be discussed with the client.

Some consultants review their planning for the job only when costs are in excess of those estimated in preparing the proposal. However, it is well to review the scope of the engagement in any case. Frequently, it may be possible to reduce the amount of work done on any specific task without seriously imperiling the validity of the data developed or conclusions reached. For example, it may have been planned to visit six branch offices. Upon close scrutiny, it may be well to plan on visiting only four of these offices to see if the results obtained justify visiting the other two.

The work of organizing the engagement should, ideally, be carried out by the man who will have day-to-day responsibility for its execution. He will then be familiar with all the steps that should be taken, and will be the logical one to hold responsible for any deviations from the plan. It is also advisable, if possible, to have this same man participate in preparing the proposal, although this is not always possible because he may be deeply involved in directing another engagement at the time the engagement is being proposed.

Carrying Out the Engagement

Even though the engagement may have been well proposed and carefully planned, carrying it out successfully is no easy matter. This involves careful attention to a number of important steps that are critical not only in developing sound recommendations but also in minimizing any disturbance to the client in carrying out the work.

A number of steps can be taken in the office before beginning work at the client premises. Probably the most important of these is to gain a thorough understanding of the client and the industry of which he is a part and background information on the principal people to be dealt with. In certain types of engagements, it is well to have someone develop the client's profit and volume statistics for the past several years, and to develop trends and compare these trends with similar statistics for the industry as a whole. These help to indicate, for example, the client's present ability to maintain his share of the market and profit per sales dollar. It is also a good idea to learn the history of the company and to study its origin, general product line, geographic dispersion, and any particular factors responsible for its past successes or failures. Much of this information can be obtained from *Moody's, Dun & Bradstreet,* and other such sources, if this is a new client. Background information on top client people, such as how long they have been working with the company, positions they have occupied either in the company or before joining the company, as well as any special interests and personality traits, should also be determined to the extent easily possible.

If possible, the consulting team should be brought together in the consultant's office so that all members can be briefed on the details of the engagement, how it is to be carried out, their role in it, and general background on the industry and company and its key people. A specific list of tasks to be performed by each man and a schedule for performing them should be given out.

A key point in the engagement is the first meeting with the client. This is where the consulting team will meet the president or other executive responsible for the engagement and his assistants. At this point, the client will carefully appraise the consultants, both in terms of their general appearance and behavior, and in how they conduct themselves and ask and answer questions. If possible, it is well to have the client executive briefly outline his understanding of the engagement and what he expects from it, and any particular requirements he will have of the consulting team. I recall one such occasion when we were told that because of religious scruples none of us would be allowed to smoke in the office but that there would be no objection if we occasionally went outside to smoke. This kind of client requirement should be brought out at this time to avoid any future annoyance to the client or embarrassment of the consultant during the engagement.

At this meeting it is also wise to make arrangements for an adequate working place. This is a step that many consultants overlook, but the proper working place is important, not only to facilitate working but also for psychological reasons. It is well for the consultants to establish their headquarters in executive territory. This indicates to all concerned, in a subtle but effective fashion, the degree of top management support given to the consulting team. I remember once interviewing a general foreman when the only office available was that of the president, who was on a trip to Europe. The general foreman indicated that this was the first time he had ever been to the president's office, and, needless to say, he knew that we were operating with the complete support of the president.

Another small but important item to be discussed at this meeting is the client personnel needed to carry out the work. This will include, as a minimum, a day-to-day contact who can be called upon to arrange interviews, obtain information, and otherwise assist in the performance of the engagement. Secretarial and filing work should be arranged for, as well as any transportation or other special facilities that might be needed.

When these matters have been taken care of, the engagement site should be toured so that all members of the consulting team can get a firsthand idea of the client's operations and meet the people responsible for them. No matter how much work has been done before, there is nothing so informative as actual on-the-site observation of the client's operations. The adequacy of the facilities, the work pace, the general calibre of the people, as well as the processes involved, are all very important in gaining an overall understanding of the client's business.

At this first meeting the first interviews should also be arranged. These will be interviews of the key people, the heads of the various areas of activities to be dealt with. As indicated earlier, it is psychologically important to interview the head of an activity (such as a vice president) before going to the men underneath him. This will enable him to provide general information regarding his sphere of operations and to indicate any particular things to be looked at. It will also enable him to arrange interviews for his subordinates.

Even after beginning scores of engagements in more or less this fashion. I still approach the first day on the job with a certain degree of trepidation, and I am always glad when it is over. The innumerable introductions to client people, their careful scrutiny of the consultants, and the need to respond intelligently to their comments and questions always strain my attentiveness and make me wish that the day was over, so that I could go back to my room at the hotel and digest all that I have learned during the day.

The work of carrying out the engagement itself boils down to essentially three things: obtaining information, analyzing information and developing recommendations, and developing the report or system.

Obtaining Information.   The needed information will be collected largely from personal interviews and from data used to supplement, augment, and verify the data collected in the interviews. Interviewing is a subject in itself, and many articles have been written about it. In essence, it is a skilled technique, which, if properly used, can be most helpful in obtaining pertinent information and all the nuances regarding it, from people who are best qualified to provide it. Interviews are often used to cross-check information obtained in other interviews.

Interviews are used to determine how things are done and what is wrong with the way things are being done, and to obtain suggestions for improvement. Lest this latter thought confuse you, I would like to point out that some of the consultants' recommendations have their origin in thoughts and ideas that they obtain from client people. It is quite logical for a consultant to consider many of the ideas prevailing within the organization, and to bring them together in the form of important recommendations. Interviewees may also include people generally knowledgeable in the field under study, professors, government officials, members of trade associations, and sometimes even competitors, along with customers and suppliers of the client organization.

A task that is almost as difficult as conducting a skillful interview is that of retaining the data obtained in the interview. Most consultants will simply take notes during the interview and augment these notes when the interview is finished. Others will tape record record the interview, although this is not too common because it tends to inhibit the interviewee as he responds to questions.

Regardless of how the interview information is preserved it must be carefully reviewed and classified so that it will be available to the consultant when he sits down and analyzes all the information he has gathered so that he can begin structuring his recommendations prior to writing the report or developing the system.

Similarly, statistical data that have been collected must be carefully analyzed to be sure that they are pertinent to the subject and that their impact is completely understood by the consultant. Sometimes the consultant will have to have data prepared especially for his needs. I remember one such instance where we asked the client to tabulate the number of units withdrawn and the number of transactions during the course of the year for each item in the inventory. This information was vitally important in determining the type of inventory control and cost accounting systems to be developed.

There are almost as many ways of organizing findings as there are consultants. Some will list important findings on 3 x 5 cards to be sorted as required. Others may use punched cards for this purpose. Some will attempt to organize pages in a notebook, and others will try to catalogue facts in their minds. The best method to be used will, of course, be determined by the type of engagement, its size and complexity, and by the size, skill, and experience of the consulting team.

An important step to be kept in mind during the fact-finding function is the interchange of data between the members of the consulting team. Normally this occurs naturally. Consultants cannot help but discuss amongst themselves any significant information they have obtained. However it is done, it is important. Because information found by one consultant in one area can significantly affect both fact-finding in other areas and conclusions in general. Failure to exchange information can often lead to conclusions that are based upon incomplete data.

In a large engagement, it is usually necessary to have regular meetings of the engagement team wherein each member summarizes for the team leader and other members of the team: what he has found, what conclusions he has drawn from his findings, and what recommendations he has in mind. This not only serves to keep the entire team informed, but it also serves as a basis for the team leader's report to the client concerning what the team is doing and what it is coming up with, a subject that is dealt with in more detail below.

Keeping accurate records of the time spent on the engagement and comparing actual time with budgeted time is vital not only to producing a profit on the engagement but also completing the engagement on schedule. On a large engagement, it is easy to think that there is plenty of time during the early stages. Therefore, good control is important from the beginning.

Another advantage of keeping good time records and comparing them with the budget is the ability to determine which areas are requiring more work than expected and to either take steps to speed up the process or explain to the client the reasons why the job is requiring more time (possibly suggesting to him the need for an additional fee to cover this work). Sometimes a delay will result from lack of cooperation by client people. This can often be rectified if brought to the attention of the client executive responsible for the engagement.

Maintaining contact with the client throughout the engagement is very important. The client wants to know what you are doing as you spend his money, and he wants to know what you are finding and whether you appear to be getting to the root of his problem. Equally important is the need to inform the client of conditions that may warrant changing the scope of the engagement. Certain areas may have to be looked at in greater detail—more offices visited, more customers talked to, more procedures reviewed. These changes can be suggested to the client at progress meetings.

Another benefit of maintaining contact with the client is that it allows the consultant to test his ideas. A client usually is very well informed about his operations, and is in a good position to intelligently evaluate the consultant's ideas while they are still in the embryo stage. He can point out either why he believes the consultant's ideas will not work or why he believes they have value. Testing ideas with the client will also tend to pre-sell him on any significant changes to be recommended. People frequently tend to resist what is strange, but when they have been exposed to an idea long enough, it begins to gain merit in their eyes. Some consultants have the philosophy that the report should never contain a surprise for the client—that all recommendations of significance should have been discussed with the client and his reactions already obtained. This is an important benefit of maintaining contact with the client.

These contacts with the client are usually of two types: formal progress reports and informal meetings. Formal progress reports are often used on large engagements, for large public or quasi-public bodies, to enable a committee or similar group to become informed regarding progress made and conditions encountered. Informal progress reporting occurs when the consulting team sits down as a group and discusses their findings and tentative thinking with the client. Or the consultant team leader may sit down with the client informally on a periodic basis, say once or twice a week, and discuss what is occurring and what the consultants are thinking. The best method to be used will, of course, depend upon the size, scope, and nature of the engagement, and the client's wishes and methods of operation. No matter how it is carried out, continuing contact with the client throughout the engagement is an essential ingredient of engagement success.

Analyzing Information and Developing Recommendations. It is difficult for the consultant to know when he has secured enough information to begin to formulate recommendations. This is where the consultant's skill and experience come into play. Probably the best determinant of the adequacy of the information is the analysis phase of the job. Some consultants tend to slight this phase and not assign adequate time and attention to it. But it is extremely important, and may well prevent the writing of progress reports that will have to be changed later, as more information comes to light.

A good analysis session requires days of free, but carefully guided, discussion among the members of the consulting team regarding the facts disclosed, their importance, and what they signify. This should serve as the basis for developing recommendations that are jointly subscribed to by all members of the team. It is at this point that the team will frequently observe that certain vital information is still needed to justify their conclusions and allow them to safely develop recommendations.

Sometimes the team leader will tend to perform the analysis function all by himself. Having obtained the findings and recommendations of each of the various members of the team, he will analyze them and formulate recommendations for the team as a whole. While this may save time, it often detracts from the quality of the work, because the conclusions are arrived at by one man rather than through a free interchange of views among the members of the team.

Developing the Report or System. The end product of the engagement is the report developed (in this context, the system can be considered the report in a systems engagement). The type of report to be issued will depend upon many factors, such as the nature of the job, type of client, nature of findings, job budget, and impact desired.

No two engagements should normally produce the same type of report, although many consultants fall into the habit of structuring each report in the same fashion. The report should be designed with the above-mentioned factors in mind, and since each of these can vary, the size, scope, format, and style of the report can vary.

In many cases, a formal written report is needed. On other occasions, an outline form of report, which the consultant explains orally, is sufficient. In some cases, visual aids are helpful; in others, only a few, well-executed charts or graphs are needed. And in some cases, particularly where confidential matters are a factor, the client wants only an oral report.

Report writing is expensive, and many consultants will allot as much as a third of the job budget to writing the report. Therefore, anything that can be done to minimize this task, without effectively destroying the impact of the facts to be reported, should be done. For a job with a limited budget, and a client, who stays close to the job, an outline type of report will often be satisfactory. A favorite method of mine is to use an overhead projector to present an outline to the client, and then give the client a copy of this outline, along with a letter of transmittal summarizing what was discussed at the meeting where the report was presented.

Consultants' reports are generally very well written. They are usually to the point, and written in an easy-to-understand fashion. Good reports are organized in a logical way, and will often make effective use of graphs and charts.

Some people speak disparagingly of consulting engagements, saying that all they ended up with was a big bound report. This may be true, in some cases, but the problem is not usually the report itself. Rather, it is the failure of the consultant to produce results that are meaningful to the client, or to carefully educate the client as to the value of following the consultant's recommendations.

Many books have been written about how to write effectively, and there is therefore no need to go into that subject in any great detail here. However, I would like to make a few suggestions to facilitate report preparation. The first is to prepare an outline. Most new consultants will want to skip this step because they are so eager to get their thoughts into writing that they are reluctant to take the time needed to develop an outline. However, developing an outline is necessary to produce a well organized report. It facilitates writing the report, because most of the consultant's thinking about what is going to be said, and how he is going to say it, is accomplished in the process of producing the outline. A report outline also makes it easy to review the report. Many people will not review a report without also having an outline. This outline enables the reader to review the report components in perspective, easily recognizing the major ideas being expressed and their relationship to each other. All in all, developing a report outline saves time for both the writer and the reviewer.

The report outline should be checked against the proposal letter to make certain that the report will cover all that was promised in the proposal. Similarly, it should also be checked against the individual findings of each man on the job, the minutes of interim review meetings, and the materials presented at these meetings. These steps will ensure that the report covers all material pertinent to the study.

Report style has already been mentioned. However, at this point I would like to emphasize the advantage of using simple, straightforward language rather than language that is intended to impress the reader with the breadth of the writer's vocabulary and his ability to use abstract terms. Also, the old saying that a picture is worth a thousand words applies particularly to reports. For this reason, it is often important to use graphs, charts, and tables to explain and amplify written or oral comments.

Most readers of consulting reports are busy men and have many demands on their time. If a report is not of vital interest to them and if it is difficult to read, they will tend to put it aside. Therefore, reports should be inviting and easy to read. They should have short sentences and paragraphs, and lots of white space on the pages, so as not to appear too forbidding or difficult to comprehend. Detailed materials should be put in an appendix whenever these details are not immediately necessary to comprehend the report. A favorite technique of mine is to use a letter of transmittal to orient the reader regarding the nature of the study and to summarize its findings. The president of a large company will often read only the letter of transmittal that accompanies the report. Therefore, this is a good vehicle for quickly acquainting him with major findings and recommendations.

My final point regarding reports deals with the report cover or binding. This should be adequate for the job, but it should not be any more formal or elaborate than necessary. It should not be designed to last for fifty years if the report may be valuable for only one or two years. However, since the report is the only part of the consultant's work that some top client people will actually see, its appearance should be pleasing to the eye, and it should reflect conscientious attention to detail and respect for the client.

Billing the Engagement

Billing is a necessary chore connected with every engagement, and the reluctance with which many consultants approach the billing of an engagement seems to indicate that this is the least desirable part of the work.

However, billing is, of course, important, and it need not be a chore or a problem if adequate arrangements have been made prior to accepting the engagement. As indicated earlier, the engagement proposal will usually indicate how the fee is to be arrived at and billed. In those instances where the client does not request a proposal, it is wise for the consultant to provide the client with a letter of understanding that indicates not only the work to be done but also the basis upon which it will be billed. I can recall in the early days of consulting for a CPA firm that some audit partners and managers were reluctant to quote a fee to the client for fear that he would not authorize the work. Whenever I accepted that premise, we almost invariably encountered problems in collecting the bill, particularly if it was a large one.

Most consulting engagements of any magnitude provide for progress billing as the work moves ahead. Large engagements for units of government, particularly, will usually specify the basis for progress payments. In other cases, this should be specified in the proposal. The format of the bill may vary, depending upon the wishes of the client and the practices of the consulting firm. Most generally, the bill will indicate the nature of the engagement and the period of time it covers. Sometimes, clients will ask for a description of the specific portions of the work being billed for. And sometimes, in very large engagements, the engagement is broken down into activities or steps, and the client is billed in accordance with work done on these activities or steps.

Progress billing has many advantages. First, it cuts down on the working capital requirements of the consultant. Many consultants would have difficulty financing a very large engagement unless they received payments as they went along. A second advantage is that it simplifies making collections, because small amounts are usually easier to collect. In addition, the consultant will have fewer problems if the client is dissatisfied, because the consultant will already have collected a part of the fee. The third, and a very important, advantage is that progress billing keeps the client aware of what the engagement is costing him, and he is therefore more inclined to appreciate the importance of the work that the consultant is doing and to provide the assistance needed to minimize the work to be done. Some consultants tend to front-end-load their billings. This means that they bill more rapidly than they earn their fee. While this improves the consultant's cash flow, and presumably saves him future collection problems, it is a form of deception and is not used by consultants who value their continuing relationship with the client.

Prompt and regular billing is important. Not only does this get your bill to the client ahead of other bills, but it also indicates a well run consulting organization. (The consultant who is confused in his administrative procedures may well be confused in his professional procedures as well.) Some consultants, however, choose to bill at strategic points of the engagement. For example, just after the conclusion of a progress meeting where the client has expressed great satisfaction with the work being done.

This, they believe—and perhaps rightfully so—facilitates the collection of their bills. It is in line with the procedure recommended by an old attorney to a young man when he said: "Bill when the tears are warmest."

However, the most important aid to collecting the fee is to do quality work. I have found many clients happy to pay a higher fee than they had expected—for highly satisfactory work. And I have seen clients who only grudgingly paid an agreed-upon fee, because they were not satisfied with the work that had been done.

Following Up on the Engagement

For many years, automobile manufacturers provided free inspection of new cars after they had been driven a few thousand miles. They did this in order to make minor adjustments to the car, if necessary, so that it would provide maximum satisfaction to the customer. The consultant should do the same. He should provide for periodic follow-up with the client, to determine the success (or any problems) that the client is having with the recommendations or systems provided by the consultant.

This procedure has a number of distinct advantages. First, it puts the client at ease when he undertakes the work, because he feels that the consultant will not just give him a report or system and then leave him to work out resulting problems by himself. Instead, the client is assured that not only will the consultant help him to resolve installation problems but he will also be practical and thorough in his recommendations, because the consultant will have to live with these recommendations as they are implemented by the client.

A second and very important advantage is one referred to earlier—by making minor adjustments in the system or recommendations, the consultant can often help the client achieve a much more successful installation of these recommendations. Clients generally see only what is wrong in the recommendations if they do not work, and do not appreciate all the good things that have gone into them. Therefore, it is important for the consultant to correct any problems as soon as possible.

Again, follow-up is also an important source of new work. The consultant, being on the premises and talking with the client management, may remind the client of other needs that the consultant can satisfy, or the consultant may observe other needs of the client and suggest additional work to satisfy these needs.

The estimated fee for the job should, if at all possible, include some time for follow-up. Many consultants have this in mind when they estimate the fee, but sometimes the time reserved for follow-up is needed for the engagement itself and the follow-up may be done at no extra fee. Some consultants believe that it is wise to avoid billing the client extra for follow-up work, since it is largely to the consultant's advantage to leave a more satisfied client and await opportunities for additional work. However, there are times when follow-up work should be billed. This occurs when additional work is required because the client did not follow recommendations in implementing the system. Usually, the client will recognize this as being his fault and will not mind being charged for the extra work required.

*   *   *

In this chapter, I have attempted to describe what I consider normal and accepted practice in carrying out certain basic types of consulting engagements. Because of the wide variety of ways in which consulting is carried on, it is quite likely that I have not touched on all aspects of practice, and I may have described certain procedures that are at variance with the way some consultants conduct an engagement. Nevertheless, I believe that this cataloguing of practice and procedures, with a few recommendations injected, should provide an effective understanding of what the consultant does in performing an engagement.

As mentioned at the beginning of this chapter, there is another type of engagement, whose end product is people. This is executive search, and in the next chapter I shall present generally followed practices in this type of engagement.

10

Executive Search Engagements

Executive search, as the name implies, is an organized search by a consulting or search firm to find a person to fill an executive position. Generally, the client rather than the executive pays for the cost of the search and all expenses connected with it. The fee charged by the search consultant is frequently a percentage of the executive's first-year salary, with a minimum fee charged in any case. IMC and many consultants do not consider executive search to be consulting. However, because of its close relationship to consulting, and because it is carried on by two large ACME firms and several CPA firms, and because relatively little has been written about its methods of operation, I am dealing with it in this book.

This type of engagement grew out of general management consulting. As new organizations and systems were developed, consultants frequently found that the client did not have the people necessary to man their organizations and systems, and therefore suggested new people. And it was only natural for the client, not knowing exactly how to proceed to obtain such people, to ask the consultant to help him find them. Consequently, many of the larger consulting firms developed executive search departments, and some of these firms still have such groups. However, as time went on, many of the people who worked in these groups left the consulting firms and established their own firms. Other full-time executive search firms have grown out of traditional employment agencies, by upgrading their skills and contacts to the executive search level.

In this chapter, I shall describe how executive search firms, or executive search departments of consulting firms, operate. Again, because of the wide disparity between firms in their methods of operation, I shall not be able to cover all aspects of all operations carried on by different firms. Before beginning to describe how the practice is carried on, however, I would like to comment briefly on some of the different types of practitioners presently working in this field. As I have already mentioned, much of this work is done by firms that spend full time in this type of activity, and a considerable amount is done by departments of general consulting firms. Recently, some large CPA firms, which for years have been informally helping their clients to find suitable candidates for top financial positions, have also organized executive search groups who operate in the same manner as full-time executive search firms. In addition, there are a number of what I might call peripheral executive search practitioners. For example, equipment manufacturers, who have been effective sources of top-level data processing talent. Usually these manufacturers charge no fee for this type of work, but they benefit in another way, by recommending people who like their equipment and are apt to continue to use it. Colleges, universities, and state employment agencies may also be said to provide executive search services, but to a very limited extent in that their services are free and generally consist of merely sorting, evaluating, and forwarding resumes to a prospective employer.

In the pages that follow, I will describe the executive search function as it is carried on by full-time executive search firms, covering such areas as: practice development, securing the engagement, conducting the search, presenting the candidates, concluding arrangements, follow-up on placed candidates, and billing for services.

Practice Development

Executive search firms use many of the same methods of practice development that are used by management consulting firms. These methods include: personal contacts, recommendations by former clients, speeches, written articles, surveys, advertising, and, in some cases, direct solicitation of engagements.

Two fruitful sources of engagements are the people placed by the search firm and the people contacted by the search firm in the course of a search. When a search firm places an executive in a top position, that executive often finds that he needs other executives to assist him, and it is only natural that he should turn to the search firm that placed him to get help in finding the executives he needs. Similarly, in searching for well-qualified candidates, experienced search people contact knowledgeable people in the industry or profession in which they are expecting to find their men. These will often be people of considerable status in their field—university professors, senior or retired executives of large well-known firms, bankers, attorneys, and CPA's. Through their contacts with these people, the search firm keeps before them the fact that it is in the search business, so that when the occasion arises, these people will either use the search firm themselves or mention it to colleagues needing these services.

Another practice development gambit is to conduct surveys on the demand for executives. One firm, which periodically conducts surveys of the variation in the number of help-wanted ads placed in newspapers as an indication of the demand for executives, has used this method very effectively. Another favorite device in getting publicity is to be mentioned in the *Wall Street Journal.* Many articles in the *Wall Street Journal* dealing with the executive job market quote people in prominent executive search firms.

Advertising is used by a number of firms, whereas direct solicitation of engagements is not very common. And, while it can hardly be considered a facet of practice development, it is interesting to note that executive search firms are sometimes hired for defensive purposes. I've been told by executive search people that some companies use a *number* of search firms, not only to find new talent but also to protect themselves from being "raided" by any of these search firms.

Securing the Engagement

Securing an executive search engagement is a much less formal procedure than securing a general consulting engagement. This stems from the fact that the fee for executive search is usually considerably smaller than for consulting, although, in a search for a president or chief operating executive of a large company, the fee may be as much as fifty thousand dollars. Most fees, however, are more likely to be in the range of ten to twenty-five thousand dollars.

Similarly, the competitive proposal is not used to any significant extent by executive search firms. Sometimes the president or other top executive of the client company will talk with one or more executive search firms to determine their capabilities and experience in searching for the kind of man the client is looking for. And, occasionally, a company will simultaneously use more than one firm to search for an executive.

The executive search firm is usually selected on the basis of such factors as its reputation, its industry expertise, its past performance, its stable of prospective candidates, and its price. Price is not usually a major consideration, however. The client wants, above all, to get the very best man for the job, one who will have the knowledge, experience, temperament, and other characteristics needed to successfully meet the requirements of the position. Thus, it is most important to employ a firm that knows how to search for this kind of man. Past experience in successfully supplying executives to a client can, of course, be particularly important.

Selection of the executive search consultant is usually followed by a letter of confirmation, prepared by the consultant and sent to the client. This letter will contain all the salient facts pertaining to the search. It will start with the basic approach to be used, and it will include the steps to be taken in developing a description of the job to be filled—describing the ideal candidate for the job and possible sources of such a candidate. It will also include a list of sources to be avoided, because either the client or the consultant is reluctant to take a man from a particular company, usually because of some existing or past close associations with that company. In addition, the letter will include provisions for determining the salary range of the position, the steps to be taken in identifying and screening candidates and presenting them to the client, and a statement of how the consultant will assist the client in making the selection from among the candidates presented. It will also provide for interim reporting to the client on the progress being made in the search, and follow-up to determine how successfully the candidate is adjusting to his new position. Finally, the letter of confirmation will also include the estimated time required to fill the position, the basis for the fee to be charged, and the charges that will be involved if the client decides, for any reason, to cancel the search once it is undertaken.

Normally the client will send a letter to the executive search firm indicating his acceptance of the conditions contained in the consultant's letter of confirmation, noting any exceptions that he wishes to make.

Conducting the Search

The first step that the consultant will take in carrying out the search is to define the position to be filled. He will determine what the company requires of this position, and the opportunities that it will offer. This determination will include such things as the job to be done, the environment in which the executive will work, the potential for future advancement, and the salary that will probably have to be paid to attract the kind of person required. The consultant will often spend some time in the client organization to determine these things, particularly if top management people are aware of the search that is going on. Sometimes the consultant will interview other people in the company to determine if any of them possess the qualifications required for the job to be filled. (I know of one case where the client was so pleased when the search department of a general consulting firm found a qualified man within the client's own company that he proceeded to give the consulting firm a number of significant general consulting engagements totaling hundreds of thousands of dollars.)

Based upon his observations of the people and the other positions in the client company, the consultant will sometimes suggest modifications in the position's duties and responsibilities so as to produce a better alignment of responsibilities within the client company, or to produce a position that can be filled more easily. After the consultant has defined the position, he will sit down with the client and request his agreement to the job specifications as the consultant has defined them.

The imaginative and enterprising search consultant can be very ingenious in developing sources of candidates, for upon this depends, to a great extent, his ability to produce the kind of executive sought. His own files contain extensive lists of people who are qualified for various types of positions. These files have been developed out of past searches and from unsolicited résumés sent in by people looking for new positions. (It should be noted, in passing, that most consultants do not make much use of unsolicited resumes, preferring, instead, to search for a man who is actually doing such a good job in his own company, and has such bright prospects there, that he is not even considering looking elsewhere.) The consultant's files will also include lists of people who have been placed in the past and who, the consultant believes, might be thinking of leaving their present employment—or might be induced to leave. (This latter possibility is, of course, quite unethical in the eyes of the better search firms.)

Finally, the files will contain lists of people who are not interested in the position themselves, but are in a good position to recommend other qualified executives.

Other sources of potential candidates are the listings of executives maintained by industry and trade associations. These listings indicate the names and positions of many people in the industry or trade. The rosters of such organizations as the Financial Executives Institute are a good example of such listings. Trade journals will also often produce names of people who appear, as a result of articles written either by or about them, to be highly successful in their field.

Universities are often good sources of people, both through the placement services that most of them maintain and through the recommendations of prominent professors concerning people knowledgeable in the professors' special areas. I have found that professors are almost always eager to recommend someone whom they believe to be especially well qualified.

Another resource of the search consultant is the wide circle of friends and acquaintances he has developed either socially or through his business contacts. For example, in the course of conducting one search, the average consultant will speak to scores of people who may also be helpful in later searches.

Having carefully checked through the various files and other sources of candidates, the search consultant will develop a list of potential candidates, as well as a list of people to call in search of candidates. With this list the consultant will begin his long series of telephone calls. In some cases the consultant will approach a potential candidate directly and explain the position to him, usually without revealing the name of the company but describing it in such a way that the candidate may be able to guess who the client is. The consultant will describe the position in considerable detail and ask the candidate if he is interested. If he is, the consultant will ask him to submit a resume for review, or, if the candidate seems to be extremely well qualified, the consultant may suggest a meeting, either in the consultant's office or in some place convenient to the candidate. If the candidate is not interested, the consultant will ask him to recommend other people who are qualified and who may be interested. The consultant may or may not contact these people, depending upon how he reacts to the candidate's description of their capabilities.

A favorite approach of the search consultant when he contacts a potential candidate is to describe the job and the qualifications of the person to fill it and ask the candidate if he knows of anyone who meets these qualifications. Frequently, as might be expected, the candidate will suggest that the consultant consider him. Sometimes a candidate will suggest other potential candidates, and, shortly thereafter upon thinking it over, will phone the consultant back and indicate that he might consider the position.

This process of contacting sources, identifying interested candidates, and approaching them goes on to the point where the search consultant may have identified as many as a dozen potential candidates. He will then begin to screen these candidates intensively. He will, of course, interview them, and many consultants will subject candidates to a battery of aptitude, personality, and psychological tests. These will be supplemented by a careful check of each candidate's references. People with knowledge of the candidate's capabilities and personality, such as former bosses, and supervisors and co-workers in his present and past places of employment will be contacted, even if they are not on the list of references provided by the candidate.

Reference-checking, like interviewing, is an art in itself. It requires the ability not only to get information but also to evaluate its source and completeness. Endorsements are subjective, depending on the nature of the person providing them, and a good search consultant must learn to "read between the lines."

Presenting the Candidates

Through the process of reference-checking and interviewing, the original list of qualified people will usually be cut down to three or four potential candidates to be presented to the client. The search consultant likes to have more than one candidate to present and likes these candidates to be well qualified technically but of different personalities, so that the consultant can determine the personality traits that most appeal to the client.

The process of presenting the candidates to the client is an interesting one. The consultant will have prepared a brochure on each of the candidates. This brochure will often include a picture, and will normally include a resume, a summary of the consultant's evaluation of the candidate's background and experience, and the results of the consultant's interviews and reference-checks. The consultant will take the client through these brochures and explain to him the pertinent features of each item. He will also generally indicate the evident desires of the candidate in terms of money, position, and working conditions, and any reservation that the candidate may have expressed regarding the company and the position to be filled.

With the candidate, the consultant will spend considerable time explaining to him the philosophy of the company environment in which he will work, and the personality traits of the executives who will screen him and either eventually employ him or reject him. He will also spend considerable time describing the characteristics of the candidate's immediate superior. In this manner, the consultant carefully prepares both candidate and client for a potential marriage between the two.

Concluding Arrangements

After the consultant has presented his candidates, he will visit the client to get his reaction to each of the candidates, and he will also visit the candidates to determine their reactions to the client. If the client indicates a specific acceptance of one or two candidates, the consultant will visit these candidates to determine if they are willing to accept the offer of the client. Problems such as salary, position, working relationships, contracts, and pension benefits are resolved at this time. If the candidates indicate their agreement to the client's terms, the client is informed of this fact. He will then eventually make an offer to one or the other of the candidates, which, hopefully, will be accepted.

If the client is not satisfied with any of the candidates, or if none of the candidates is willing to work for the client, the consultant must then continue the search and produce new candidates until he eventually finds one who is satisfactory to the client and is willing to work for him.

Sometimes, for various unexplained reasons, no candidate is acceptable to the client. Or sometimes the client's reputation for firing previous employees is so bad that it is not possible for the consultant to find an acceptable candidate for the job. Normally, however, this latter condition will be discovered by the consultant before he has proceeded very far in the search.

Follow-up on Placed Candidates

After the client has hired an executive candidate, the thorough-going search consultant will visit both the client and the executive to observe how things are working out.

Any problems or reservations mentioned by either party can be discussed with the party concerned or diplomatically mentioned to the other party, so that they can be taken care of before they become acute sources of dissatisfaction.

This is an important aspect of the search consultant's work since some search firms guarantee to replace an executive who leaves within six months, or a year, of employment. Therefore, it is to the consultant's distinct benefit to see that his candidate works out on the job. If he does not, the consultant must again go through the search process and again present qualified candidates for the position.

Billing for Services

As indicated earlier, search consultants charge the client for their services. These charges usually cover the fee and all expenses such as telephone, travel, psychological tests, and similar items. The fee is usually a percentage of the first year's compensation, with certain minimums for relatively low salary positions and, occasionally, maximums for extremely high salary positions.

Normally the consultant will bill the client monthly for expenses incurred and possibly for a portion of the fee, even though he has no assurance that he will produce an acceptable candidate and thus earn his fee. By billing a standard hourly rate as the search proceeds, the consultant insures himself against an abrupt or arbitrary cancellation by the client. It sometimes happens, for example, that the client is debating in his own mind about promoting persons in his firm and merely wants to compare them with the outside talent produced by the consultant. If the client decides to promote in-house people and cancel the search, the consultant is still paid for his time up to that point.

In cases where the consultant fails to produce a marriage after a reasonable time, the search consultant will resign from the engagement and usually will bill the client for time and expenses incurred in the search.

*   *   *

Having discussed the methods used in both general consulting firms and executive search firms, I shall continue, in the next chapter, with a discussion of the personal and professional characteristics of a good consulting staff.

11

Building a
Consulting Staff

Perhaps it is because of the challenge that the work offers, or because of the pleasure that we all get from imparting suggestions to others, but, for whatever reason, there are apparently a great number of people who want to become consultants. This means that consulting firms are usually in a good position to be very selective in building their consulting staffs—and they are. A review of the functions carried out by the consultant and the various technical and psychological requirements for successfully providing these functions cannot help but indicate the importance of a competent staff to the success of a consulting firm. Therefore, in building a consulting staff there are a number of factors to be considered: personal characteristics, consulting experience, background and training, career goals, and the process of putting all this together.

Personal Characteristics

Good consultants are hard to find because of the many qualities needed to succeed in the profession. A good consultant must possess the following attributes to a considerable degree: Intelligence, Confidence, Curiosity, Creativity, Energy, Tact, Persistence, and Diplomacy. Finding a man or woman with all of these qualities, at least to an acceptable degree, is difficult.

While most of these requirements are self evident, one or two deserve special attention—curiosity and creativity, for example. A person who is not curious about the workings of everything around him will tend to overlook facts that may have a major impact on what he is studying. Similarly, unless the consultant is creative, he cannot develop a new concept, a new approach, or a new technique in handling the client's activities. The development of PERT as a means of improving control over the development and production of the Polaris missile is an excellent example of the use of creativity on a consulting engagement.

Energy, tact, persistence, and diplomacy are all very important attributes, particularly in getting a client to adopt recommendations. Without these characteristics the consultant will often be unsuccessful.

However, the very qualities that make a good consultant often make that consultant a little difficult to handle. Because good consultants are intelligent, curious, creative, and energetic, they dislike routine and close supervision. They like to do things in their own way, on their own schedule, and at their own speed. I recall an extreme instance where a consultant's "artistic temperament" got a little out of hand. Late in the afternoon, he had been given an assignment to write an article. The next morning, the partner asked the consultant how he was doing. The consultant replied that he had only started that morning, saying, "You know that I can't be creative late in the afternoon." Needless to say, most consultants are "pros," and go about their work in a much more disciplined and business-like manner.

Good consultants are also restless people. They tire easily of doing the same thing in the same location. They welcome the changes that a never ending series of engagements can provide. This makes them interesting people, but it also produces a rapid turnover in the consulting profession. Naturally, supervising a group of people such as this is not an easy task.

Consulting Experience

In addition to the personal characteristics discussed above, a consultant requires at least two types of skills. First, he must have technical knowledge in a particular discipline such as marketing, EDP, or organization. This, of course, is the cornerstone of his career. Many people, including some people who wish to run consulting firms, believe that this is really all that is required. They forget one other very important requirement—a first-hand knowledge of how the consulting practice itself is carried on (i.e., conversance with all the various steps required to obtain engagements, to structure them, and to carry them out successfully).

Technical knowledge is important but it is usually not enough, by itself, to ensure a successful job. In rare instances, the ability of a consultant to acquaint the client with new or better ways of doing things is all that the client needs to enable him to take the idea and run with it. For the most part, however, the consultant must do much more—and this is where his consulting experience comes into use.

Consulting experience is required, first of all, for appraising the job environment and developing the proposal. The consultant must know if the client is really interested in making improvements, and whether he is in a position to make any changes that may be necessary to bring about these improvements. If these conditions are not present, an experienced consultant will often decline to submit a proposal.

Consulting experience is also necessary to properly structure the job. Knowing how to identify problems and how to find their causes is, in itself, a major task. A consultant must know what to look for, where to look for it, and how (and how deeply) to penetrate the various areas affecting a problem. He must know how to estimate the time required to do the job, and the skills required to do it.

In addition, he must know when to recommend changes in the scope or nature of the approach, or even when to abandon an approach altogether. Sometimes, after a short period on an engagement, the consultant will find that the problem is other than he has been led to expect. I recall such an instance, when after a few weeks of preliminary study, the partner in charge of the job asked to talk with the president of the company. His message to the president was:

> We have looked around your shop a bit and we think we've found the problem. In essence the problem is you. You just don't seem to have what it takes to effectively run this company. But you have most of your money tied up in it, and if it continues to operate as it has in the past, it may become bankrupt and you'll lose all your money. Therefore, I suggest that you bring in someone else to run your business, and that

you take the profits from it and live comfortably without having to work.

The client accepted this recommendation and the company was saved. But, surely, it takes an experienced consultant not only to recognize these conditions but also to have the courage and the ability to deal with them so effectively.

What consultants refer to as "client handling" is extremely important. This covers all the psychological aspects of gathering information, convincing people that change is necessary, and motivating them to change, in spite of their innate tendencies to maintain the *status quo*. It often takes a real measure of courage to tell the chief executive of a client company what he does not want to hear. I was involved in a classic example, where the client company was losing money and the president kept refusing to act on our recommendations, which were designed to stop these losses. Finally, we had to go to him and explain that we thought he had only three choices: (1) he could implement our recommendations and, hopefully, turn his company around; (2) he could sell his company; or, (3) he could do nothing (which, in our opinion, would lead to disaster). The president listened attentively to what we had to say, and then agreed to make the changes we suggested. The subsequent success of his firm, turned him into a loyal and enthusiastic supporter of our services.

Knowing how to handle such clients (i.e., those who are difficult to get along with, who resist changes, or are naturally suspicious of consultants) requires a great deal of tact as well as consulting experience. Motivating people to want to change their methods is often more difficult than determining the types of changes that are needed. A consultant who is not experienced in this respect will find it difficult to succeed.

Similarly, the ability to develop clear and straightforward reports and carefully structured charts, graphs, and diagrams greatly simplifies the task of explaining to the client the nature of his problems and what needs to be done to solve them.

Clearly, then, a great deal more is required of a consultant than pure technical knowhow. Recognition of this fact is one of the reasons for the continued success of many old established consulting firms.

Background and Training

Consultants come from a number of backgrounds. Industry, government, teaching, and the graduating classes of colleges and universities are the usual sources. People from all these areas will usually come equipped with technical knowhow, and it is up to the consulting firm to teach them the art of consulting. While many business schools, for example, will touch upon consulting in their curriculum, to the best of my knowledge there is no "how to do it" course available in any school. Therefore, this training must be provided by the consulting firm itself.

Probably the most difficult of these people to prepare for consulting work are the recent college graduates, who lack experience both in their technical fields and in consulting. Nevertheless, some of the larger consulting firms have been employing MBA's directly from school. They apparently have the ability to fit these people into consulting teams so that they gain experience as part of a group without being in a position to make critical mistakes. These young MBA's, given the proper experience, can become first rate consultants—but it takes a large firm, working on large engagements, to be able to absorb these people into consulting teams so that they can gain the experience needed to do professional consulting work.

The most common practice is to take bright young men or women who have had three to five years of experience after leaving school and train them as consultants. Not only will they have technical knowledge, but they will also have had experience in administration. They will know the innerworkings of a company and the problems of a supervisor, and thus will have more understanding and sympathy for the difficulties that a supervisor encounters in his day-to-day work.

Keeping current in their chosen disciplines is a major problem for consultants. In areas such as EDP, for example, change is so rapid that a consultant who does not have constant exposure to these changes will soon be out of date. Thus, if a firm wants to keep its consultants in top form, it must provide them with the opportunity, either on the job or otherwise, to keep themselves up-to-date in their special areas of expertise. Some firms spend considerable amounts of money to do this.

Other firms, however, spend very little on training. They tend to recruit people who are current in their chosen disciplines and to keep them only so long as they manage to remain current. When the time comes that they are no longer up-to-date in their field, these firms let them go. This is a rather cold way of dealing with people, but the endless group of applicants for the consulting profession permits some firms to do this.

The discipline of consulting itself does not change as rapidly as the technical disciplines with which it deals. Therefore, once the consultant reaches the supervisory level in his firm, his keeping current in any of those disciplines is not so important as before. As a consultant moves up to a supervisory position and directs a team comprised of specialists in several disciplines, he becomes more of a generalist. He gets to know the basic principles involved in a number of disciplines but ends up as master of only one—the discipline of consulting.

Career Goals

Only a small percentage of all consultants make a lifetime career of the profession. Many entrants into the profession do not intend to stay long. Some are not suited to, or do not like, the work. Others find the travel demands so heavy as to interfere with family life, and still others leave because they feel that the work places more demands on them than they wish to cope with.

A major reason for consultants to leave a consulting firm is to accept a position with a client for whom they have done consulting work. Consultants are paid well but only moderately so. Consultants can often earn more in a position with a client company than they do in their own firm.

Moreover, consulting provides good training and is a good stepping stone to other, more lucrative jobs. Many young people plan to spend only a year or two in consulting, for the training that it will give them, and then proceed to find a line position in the outside world. However, it usually takes one or two moves in the business world before a consultant is able to settle down and work in the more highly structured environment of a line-type position.

For consultants who move up through the ranks and become partners, principals or vice-presidents in their companies, the financial rewards are great. These are the people who share in the profits, and a well-established consulting firm should be quite profitable. However, consulting places heavy demands on them. The need to constantly develop new work and to respond to the vacillating demands of clients, plus the unusually heavy travel demands of this type of work, place a heavy burden on the physical well-being of the consultant. For this reason, many consulting firms have a mandatory retirement age of 60, because if a man is not in full vigor he may find it difficult to meet the heavy demands of an executive position in a consulting firm.

Proper Staffing

Building a consulting staff requires a balancing of the firm's needs against the talent available. In all consulting firms, the need for staff will vary considerably, both in size and in discipline, from time to time. The volume and nature of the work received will, of course, affect these needs considerably. In this respect, a firm that specializes in large engagements, such as those required by units of government, will have a much more difficult time keeping a balanced workload than one specializing in small engaments, which seem to flow in a more constant volume. Not only will the volume of work change, but also the skills required to staff engagements received can change. An idle EDP man cannot be substituted for an industrial engineer, or an accountant for a marketing man. This means that while one set of consultants whose skills are greatly in demand at the moment may be putting in a considerable amount of overtime, another set of consultants, with other skills, may be unassigned.

To be caught "on the bench" so to speak is considered dangerous to the consultant's tenure with the firm, and consultants tend to do whatever they can to avoid this fate. Sometimes they will even spend more time than necessary on existing engagements and thus increase the cost of engagements in progress. As a result, proper staffing is second only to adequate work volume in determining the profitability of a consulting firm.

Unfortunately, it often takes more than a crystal ball to successfully forecast the type and timing of future engagements, and, thus, providing a balanced, fully utilized staff at all times is extremely difficult. Staffing up in advance of an anticipated engagement is a good way to lose money. Similarly, holding consultants for specific jobs that are expected, rather than assigning them to jobs that are presently available, is also costly. A well established consulting firm can often overcome some of these peaks and valleys in the workload by delaying the start of engagements—thus creating a buffer, or "surge-tank." This permits the firm to await the arrival of staff from other engagements. Engagements can often be deferred up to 90 days without seriously endangering them, but beyond this, there is a good chance that the client will either decide not to have the work done after all or will ask someone else to do it. Thus, this technique, while helpful, has its limitations.

* * *

In this chapter I have tried to provide some insight into the personal and professional characteristics that a consulting firm takes into consideration when selecting its consulting staff, and the reasons why these characteristics are important to the success of both the consultant and the firm. In doing so, I believe I have also shed some light on the profession as a career.

In the next chapter, I shall take a look at the foreign market for consulting services.

12

The Foreign Market

Viewed in its broadest terms, where consulting is considered as just one man advising another, consulting has been practiced wherever one man could communicate with another, and from the beginning of civilization.

However, viewed in the context of this book, consulting only began to be practiced around the beginning of the twentieth century—principally in the United States, Canada, and Great Britain. The development of consulting in these countries was a natural result of certain conditions that existed there to a much greater extent than in most other countries. Chief among these conditions that were favorable to the evolution and growth of consulting were:

A rapidly advancing technology
The increasing cost of labor
The growth of large companies
The use of professional managers, and
The availability of a means of measuring corporate and
    managerial performance (i.e., the ability, through the use
    of accounting and statistical summarization and report-

ing procedures, to determine how well companies and their managers are doing and to compare these results with those being achieved by other companies and other managers).

These factors, which also promoted the growth of business and the development of new management and production techniques, along with measures of their effectiveness, enabled these countries to achieve great heights in the production of goods and services. These capabilities were visibly demonstrated during World War II, and thus, when World War II was over, it was only natural for other countries to want to follow the production and management examples of these countries, particularly the United States.

One opportunity to do so grew out of the Marshall Plan for the revitalization of European industry and MacArthur's program to modernize and rebuild Japan. These programs resulted in the exportation of U. S. machinery and equipment and, with it, the knowhow to operate the modern plants being built in the war-devastated countries.

Other opportunities arose with the overseas expansion of U. S. companies. Whereas only a handful of U. S. companies had any significant operations overseas before World War II, after the war many large manufacturing companies established manufacturing facilities in foreign countries. This foreign expansion occurred largely in countries that did not possess American production and management knowhow. This, in turn, required Americans to go overseas to manage and run these new plants, and eventually train local people to replace American personnel. Many companies used consultants for these efforts, and thus people in these countries were not only able to see tangible results of American knowhow but were also able to observe at first-hand and learn the practices that underlay this knowhow.

And the work that U. S. consulting firms did overseas gave most of these firms a base for establishing permanent operations in these countries. These bases have been retained and, in many cases, expanded so that a number of large U. S. consulting firms are now doing close to half of their total volume of work overseas. This makes the foreign market an important segment of consulting work, and I shall use the remainder of this chapter to discuss this market, as it now exists and as I believe it may be expected to exist over the next decade or two.

Location of the Market

Every nation—the developed as well as the developing countries—can be considered a potential market for consulting services. While the need for consulting is not so acute in the developed countries (U. S., Canada, England, and Europe, for example), it does exist there. A great amount of consulting work is needed just to keep companies in these countries abreast of new developments in technology and management. As I discuss in Chapter Thirteen, I believe that there will continue to be a large market for consulting services in the United States, and so it is reasonable to expect that there will be a similar, if not greater, need for consulting in other developed nations. This work will be needed not only to keep business and industry up-to-date, but also to help governments become more efficient and effective in dealing with today's (and tomorrow's) numerous social problems.

In the developing countries, there is a very great need to catch up (and then, of course, to stay abreast). As one who has traveled in many developing countries (often replete with natural resources and with people who are intelligent and well intentioned) and has seen the limited production of even the basic necessities of life, I have become acutely aware of what the introduction of better production and management techniques could do for such countries. And having witnessed the miraculous development of Japan over the last 30 years, as a result of the introduction of better ways of doing things, I am convinced that, given the right environment in which to work, consulting could do a great deal to improve the lot of undeveloped nations.

Thus, it seems only fair to say that a potential market for consulting exists in *every* nation in the world. The conditions necessary to permit the effective rendering of consulting services in these areas, and the obstacles to be overcome, as well as the assets already present and waiting to be utilized, are discussed below.

Nature of the Market

I have already indicated to some degree the difference between developed and developing nations as a potential market for consulting services. Therefore, in discussing the nature of this market, I will retain this distinction.

Developed Nations. It is difficult to draw the line between developed and developing nations. There is no easy line of demarcation, and the decision of where to draw the line is an arbitrary one at best. This decision is further complicated by the question of what factors to consider when we are determining what constitutes development—industrial, political, social, educational, religious, or artistic? The most commonly used factor in making this determination is industrial development, and so I shall use it here as the deciding factor.

To start with, the consulting needs of all other industrial nations can be considered to be at least as great as, and similar to, those of the United States, Canada, and Britain. As I mentioned earlier, in this country there is still a need to fine-tune the productive facilities and management techniques of companies that are not quite up-to-date, and to disseminate new concepts and practices as they develop. There is also the need to extend to government, institutions, and services the practices that have been found effective in running industrial companies. But in other industrialized nations, these facilities and techniques are not so well developed as they are in the United States, and many of the large industrial corporations are family-managed, or managed by people chosen for reasons other than demonstrated managerial capability. In addition, the concept of management responsibility to shareholders is not so well developed as it is in the U. S. Thus, there is still a great deal to be done in such countries.

Another factor to be dealt with is the changing attitude of employees toward their work, both in the United States and other developed countries. Employees are no longer satisfied to just have a job, or to have a job that pays well. They also want to have a job that has meaning, where they can see and appreciate what they have accomplished. In effect, they want their jobs enriched. This desire must be dealt with and accommodated, where possible, in many developed countries.

Developing Countries. Developing countries, for the most part, need consulting services of a more basic type. Except for rare companies operated by progressive nationals or by foreigners, companies in developing nations need to learn the basic skills of how to design, produce, and market products and services, how to manage these efforts, and how to measure what has been accomplished. Even in a relatively well developed country like Brazil, so basic a thing as product design is greatly in need of improvement. It is hard, for example, to find a manually operated can opener that is as easy to use as those we were using in the United States before the advent of electric can openers.

Similarly, product quality needs to be improved. Metals are usually too soft or otherwise inferior, products are not standardized, and product safety is often ignored. Continuous availability of what should be a standard product, such as plain bond paper, cannot always be relied upon. Marketing is weak. Stores cannot be counted upon to keep items in stock, product guarantees are poor or nonexistent, storekeepers are indifferent, and the prerogative of returning a product that doesn't fit or is otherwise unsatisfactory is largely unheard of. (I remember a time in one of these countries when my wife wanted to buy a pair of shoe laces in a shoe store. The clerk told her they had none. My wife then pointed to some shoes on display and asked if she could buy the laces out of those shoes, thinking that this might be possible because some of the new shoes had no laces. The clerk refused to do this, and my wife ended by buying a pair of shoes just to get the laces.)

In addition, mail and telephone communications are erratic, causing streets to be full of messengers delivering documents and messages that should go by mail or telephone. Transportation is slow, hazardous, and expensive. Banking practices are complex, inflexible, and expensive, and laws are archaic and cumbersome. Weak, ineffective, bureaucratic, and sometimes corrupt governments often hinder business more than they help it. Employees, from the lowest worker level to top management, are largely untrained. In many countries, employee health and safety and labor-saving equipment are sadly lacking, and, usually, the only employee benefits paid are those dictated by the government.

The situation is most desperate in countries that are not exporting large quantities of high-priced raw materials and therefore must use scarce foreign exchange to buy needed petroleum and other expensive raw materials. Not so desperate, but still demanding attention, are the requirements of the new "have" nations, which are selling petroleum and other raw materials at double and triple former prices and therefore have huge surplus revenues that they need help in disposing of to good advantage.

Obviously, developing countries offer a fertile field for consulting work. Given full rein, consultants ought to be able to find more work in these countries than they can ever hope to handle. The problem is—how do they go about satisfying this need?

Supplying the Market

There is no doubt that a foreign market for consulting services does in fact exist, particularly in developing countries. The problem for the U.S. consultant is how to supply that market, a process I shall try to describe below.

In foreign countries, just as in the United States, the major steps in a consulting engagement are: obtain the work, staff the job, perform the engagement satisfactorily, collect the fee, and, an additional step for foreign work, convert the fee into a currency that the consultant can use.

Obtaining the Work. The sources of work are numerous—foreign or multi-national companies, local companies, local governments, and local entities where the work is suggested by and financed through international or regional lending agencies, such as the World Bank, the United Nations, or Export-Import Bank. The consultant need not even have an office in, or be known in, the country in which he wishes to work. In certain cases, such as where the work is done for a foreign or multi-national company, or where it is sponsored by an international lending agency, the work can often be arranged in the native country of the consultant. He can persuade the U.S.-based head office of a foreign or multi-national company that he can help their foreign subsidiary. Or, he can convince the lending agency that his is the best qualified firm to help the borrower.

However, if the consultant is to get any great number of engagements in a country, he will usually have to open an office in that country, or arrange to be represented there. This will permit him to sell *local* management of the foreign or multi-national company on his ability to help them. And then he can sell head-office management on the idea, if that proves to be necessary (and often it isn't). And, certainly, if the consultant is to do any amount of work for local business and (usually) local governments, it is better if he is located in, and known in, the country where he wants to work. Thus, the consultant has to be willing to make a commitment, usually somewhat expensive, if he intends to exploit the foreign market to any great degree. This commitment will entail having a representative in the country who is (or will be) known, who understands the country and knows how people think and act, and who understands the language.

(In cases of highly technical services, where the technology itself is critical and not widely understood, translators can be used if needed.)

Staffing the Job. Once the engagement is secured, the first real problem is to staff the engagement. The natural thing is to think of sending staff from the consultant's native country. This seems easy, since he already employs, or at least knows, people who have the skills needed, and many people express a desire to work in a foreign country. However, the task of obtaining people (including spouses and children) who have suitable personalities, the ability to speak the language, and the basic skills needed, is not easy. It is expensive to uproot, transport, and relocate individuals or families and their belongings. Passports, visas, and medical check-ups in the home country, and customs clearances, living accommodations, and educational facilities in the foreign country are all expensive, time-consuming, and frustrating to obtain.

Third-country nationals are often a good source of consulting talent, particularly if they know the language to be used, and, better yet, are already living in the foreign country where the work is to be done. Often these people cost less and understand the native people better, even though they might not be so proficient technically. The work to be done in the foreign market will not usually require the highest degree of technical skill anyway, since it is often a case of teaching the client to "walk before he runs."

It is sometimes possible to find people native to the country where the work is to be done who have the basic skills required. They will, of course, know the language, the people, and their customs. Often these people have been educated in the U.S. and would like to return to their native country, or have already returned and not been able to find a job that will fully utilize their training. And sometimes it is possible to find well trained native people who have already used their technical training working as employees of a local company or acting as consultants in their field. This, of course, is a relatively rare occurrence, and these people should be snapped up if they can otherwise meet the qualifications of the consulting firm.

Performing the Engagement. Carrying out the work can, in itself, be a demanding experience for the resident head of the consulting group, particularly if he is a stranger to the country. In many cases the client will never have used a consultant before and he will not know how to use the consultant or what to expect from him. Usually the client will expect too much, believing that somehow the consultant will give him a finished product with no effort on his part. Or the client may be overly suspicious of the consultant, because he (the client) is not used to working with foreigners. And finally, the client may not understand the consultant—he may understand the consultants' language but not the technical terms or concepts expressed. As a result, a great many more meetings and reports will be needed than in a typical domestic engagement.

For the client to obtain lasting benefits from the engagement, it will usually be necessary to train his people in the new systems developed. This, too, usually requires more work than in a domestic engagement. The people to be trained will often lack the basic skills or aptitudes usually found among workers at the same level in the U.S. They will often feel ill at ease working with a foreign consultant and will pretend to know more than they do and will be afraid to ask questions. There may also be a language problem, not only of words, but also of concepts and practices as well. Thus, it will take much longer to select and train people as workers than it would in the U. S. In this regard, I remember one foreign engagement where we were running schools to train people to assist us in the work to be done. We trained well over a hundred people but were never able to get any of them to assist us on the project or to run the systems we had developed. It turned out that these people had never had any intention of leaving their present jobs, and had only attended the training class in order to get the certificate we would give them.

Collecting and Converting the Fee. Often when work is financed by parent companies or lending agencies having access to "hard" currency, the consultant can arrange to receive all or part of his fees in such currency. This should be arranged before the contract is entered into. Otherwise, while the client may be willing to pay in local currency, the consultant may have difficulty in converting these payments into dollars or other freely convertible currency. Sometimes the local central bank can and will do this, but sometimes the consultant will end up with local currency that he must spend locally, either to expand his practice or, possibly, to buy things for export (which often gives rise to a whole new set of problems— I still have a pair of shoes I bought to help use up a friend's blocked currency).

Another potential problem that is often overlooked is local taxes—both on the consulting firm and on the people it brings into the country. Usually both are subject to local taxes, particularly if the contract runs for a year or more. Sometimes, as where the tax status is in doubt, it is possible to get the client to reimburse the consultant for taxes levied upon the consulting firm and its non-resident employees.

Foreign consulting can be successful, satisfying, and profitable, but it requires a great deal of knowledge about the conditions to be encountered and a great deal of pains-taking care in planning, staffing, and carrying out the engagement to make it so.

The Future

With all the management and production improvements that are needed in foreign countries, particularly developing ones, it is natural to conclude that the future of consulting in the foreign market is indeed bright. In total it is. But as in many other cases, the foreign market will be captured and dominated by those who are best prepared to enter it. In appraising the potential of this market, it is well to remember that it can be supplied not only by U. S. firms but also by firms outside the U. S. such as third-party nationals and firms native to the countries to be served.

A number of other countries have consulting firms equally well trained and experienced, or nearly so. In addition, these firms and their employees are often more conditioned to, and more experienced in, working in foreign countries than U. S. firms and people; their fees and salaries are usually lower, and, equally important, their knowledge of other languages is usually greater.

In addition to these "outside" firms, there are local firms native to the countries to be served. Some of these are comprised of native people trained abroad who have worked for U. S. or other consulting firms, either abroad or in their native country, and some represent international firms whose talent resources they can draw upon. Their knowledge of local people and their language and customs will often make up for any lack of technical expertise. Sometimes their salary scales are lower than those of U. S. firms, and they don't need to bear the cost of importing consultants from abroad. Somewhat surprisingly though, because of the limited number of trained people in a developing country, the salaries of local consultants are often higher than those of U.S. or English consultants. I remember the head of a Brazilian consulting firm telling me that he could hire U.S. consultants cheaper than Brazilian ones, and that English consultants were even less expensive.

In summary, the foreign market for consulting is big—much bigger than the domestic market. But like the foreign market for commodities and for other services, it is not just there for the taking. This market will be penetrated profitably only by those consultants who either have a very specialized, highly prized service to provide, or by those who fully understand all the ramifications and complexities of the foreign market and are willing to commit the time, talent, and money necessary to cope with these requirements on a long-term basis.

* * *

Having explored the realities and possibilities of consulting abroad, let us now turn to the future and see what our crystal ball has to tell us about the general prospects for management consulting in the United States during the last quarter of this century.

13

The Future of Consulting

There are many factors that tend to influence the future of consulting, and I shall now present my evaluation of these factors in terms of their impact on the consulting profession.

To begin with, I believe that there will be a continuing demand for consultants' services. In general management, for example, organization studies, general surveys, long-range planning, and top management appraisal are all areas where the outside objectivity of the consultant will continue to be needed in both large and small organizations.

In addition, continuing advancements in technical states of the art, and widespread dissemination of information covering these advancements will lead many companies to seek the specialized knowhow of consultants knowledgeable in these disciplines and techniques. Some large companies may be in a position to use internal expertise in these areas, but many of the medium-sized and most of the smaller companies will not, since they will not be able to spare qualified people from their regular duties to undertake such special projects. Thus, there should be a considerable amount of work for consultants in appraising a company's need for these new techniques and in installing them.

The EDP field should continue to offer opportunities for large amounts of work. Many college students are learning about and using computers, and thus nearly every company should have a great deal of in-house general knowledge of computers in the future. While this may cut down the assistance needed from consultants in selecting, installing, and implementing computer equipment, it will also provide a generation of top executives who are well aware of the assistance they can get from computers in such areas as financial and operational planning and who will rely on consultants for guidance in these areas.

The growth of service industries will certainly give rise to a respectable volume of work, not only because of this growth but also because of the absence of measurement and control in many of these services. Consultants will be needed to help develop effective control measures in these areas and to assist management in adopting them.

The rapid and continuing growth of government and the inherent reasons (political, legal, and manpower) for government to use consultants will certainly provide a large market for consulting services. These engagements may not be so profitable nor so predictable as consultants would like, but the work should be there for them to go after.

Government regulations in areas of consumer and employee protection, environmental improvement, and use of scarce commodities will provide a sizable amount of consulting work. This will be in essentially two areas: (1) providing the knowhow needed by companies to meet the new standards imposed, and (2) providing the data called for by these regulations. The first may involve engineering consultants more than management consultants, but developing and providing the data called for in the second area is clearly within the scope of management consulting.

How will these opportunities affect the demand for people in the profession? As long as the profession continues to exist and there is a turnover of its people, there will be a continuing demand for new consultants. Even without growth, consulting firms would still need new people to replace those who leave the profession. However, the profession should grow, and grow significantly in certain areas. Perhaps this growth will not be so great as in the past, but growth should be there—especially in government services and the newer disciplines.

In particular, there should be an expanded need for people with technical knowhow in new disciplines, as, for example:

Health care
Environmental controls
Employee motivation
Resource utilization
Governmental planning and control
Planning and controlling of service industries.

People who are interested in getting into consulting work will probably find it easier to enter the profession if they will gain some in-depth experience in any of these disciplines. Consulting firms will require people with these capabilities in order to provide services to their clients in these new and expanded areas. On the other hand, there will be less demand, or at least not a significantly increased demand for people skilled in the more traditional fields of consulting. Thus, a young man or woman interested in getting into consulting work might well become a specialist in one or another of the new disciplines and so become an attractive candidate for employment by a consulting firm.

Summary

In summarizing the future of the consulting profession, certain things seem to be self-evident. The first of these is that consulting will continue. The need for objective appraisal, the need for specialized new talents, the need for quick and competent assistance, and the need for government and institutions to carry out their newly expanded roles, all will continue to produce a significant demand for consulting services.

Added to this, of course, are the numerous new disciplines that will develop with the growth of the economy. This growth will be stimulated by the tremendous educational expenditures and efforts in the United States today, which are producing a highly skeptical, inquisitive, and well-informed group of young people entering the work force. These new disciplines should provide solid work opportunities for the consulting profession.

However, we must recognize that as times change, employment conditions change, and employee aspirations and motivations change, many of the existing disciplines and services provided by consultants will become less and less important.

Consulting firms, naturally, will have to react to these changes in demands. However, this is not likely to be a problem, because consultants are traditionally a very flexible, versatile, and ingenious group of people. If they are not able to make these types of changes, they really do not have any business being in their respective places in the economic system.

One final point of interest, particularly to the young person planning on getting into consulting work, is that a good way to enter the profession is through knowledge and experience in these newer disciplines. This, when added to the native capabilities, disposition, desires, and tendencies required to be a consultant should produce a well qualified candidate for a consulting career. The individual who has these basic capabilities and is willing to acquire specialized knowledge in these newer fields as a stepping stone to entering consulting should find consulting a challenging and rewarding experience, and one that will absorb all the effort that he wishes to devote to it.

APPENDIX

Description of Specific Consulting Activities

GENERAL MANAGEMENT

Organization Studies

Determining the positions required in an entity, their relation to each other, and the duties and responsibilities of each.

General Surveys

Evaluating all facets of an entity: its purpose, potential, and future; and the people, organization, and methods used to achieve its goals.

Long-Range Planning

Evaluating the goals and potential of an entity and its plans to achieve those goals; and making suggestions for facilitating the achievement of its goals (or modifying them, if this seems appropriate).

Top Management Appraisal

Evaluating the strengths and weaknesses of individual members of top management to determine the capacity of each to fulfill the requirements of his present

position and to be promoted to positions of greater
responsibility.

Executive Compensation

Determining the appropriate salary grade and range
for executives in line with salaries paid for comparable
responsibilities elsewhere in the market area for such
executives and in line with salaries paid to other executives in that entity.

Executive Search

Finding a person to fill a specific position in an organization. This usually also involves determining the
proper duties and responsibilities of the position, the
requirements of the person to fill it, and the appropriate salary range. This activity is described more
fully in Chapter Ten.

PRODUCTION

Plant Layout

Determining the most efficient arrangement of facilities within a plant to achieve the most effective use
of people and equipment and the best flow of materials
through the plant.

Production Methods

Determining the best combination of people, equipment, and work methods to produce a product or
service.

Time Studies

Determining the expected time required to perform a specific operation in the production of a product or service. These studies can be combined to determine the expected time to produce the whole product or service. The studies can be based upon actual observation of workers, or they can be constructed from tables of predetermined times for the various component movements needed to perform an operation—reach, grasp, turn, etc.

Production Scheduling

Establishing schedules to most efficiently meet production requirements, bearing in mind desired completion dates and all potential restraints on production, such as availability of material, people, equipment, etc., and modifying these schedules as conditions change.

Inventory Control

Developing a system to assure, within desired limits, the availability of items, or component parts thereof, needed to carry on the activities of an organization and to minimize the quantity on hand, in line with volume and frequency of demand, replenishment times and costs, and costs to own and store the item.

Materials Handling

Determining the best methods to use in moving and storing the commodities used or produced in an operation. Often this speciality overlaps, or relates closely to, plant layout or production methods.

Equipment Maintenance

Developing systems to assure adequate and least-cost maintenance of facilities, to minimize breakdowns, and to assure maximum efficiency in the use of people, supplies, and equipment.

Plant Safety

Determining potentially hazardous conditions in a location, and methods to use to minimize or eliminate these hazards; also, developing safety programs to use in training workers to identify and avoid potentially hazardous conditions or acts.

MARKETING

Market Analysis

Determining the potential or actual market for a product or service, and the way in which to penetrate that market.

Sales Forecasting

This is akin to market analysis, but usually refers to products or services already being marketed, and it is in more detail. Sales forecasting usually involves a projection of the volume of sales expected for each type of product or service—usually by market territory. It is used to plan marketing activities and activities for the organization as a whole.

Distribution Methods

Determining the most efficient method to use in distributing the product sold. It extends to channels of distribution (dealers, jobbers, etc.), as well as to ways in which to transport the product (warehouse, direct shipment, dealer's stock, etc.).

Sales Compensation

Determining the most effective way to compensate salesmen—salary, salary and commission, bonus, etc. Often, this will involve setting sales quotas and other bases for determining compensation.

FINANCE

Accounting Systems

Developing and installing systems used to effectively and accurately record financial transactions in books of account so as to be able to determine the results of operations, assist in controlling assets and costs, and provide data needed to file reports with government and regulatory bodies. Usually, accounting systems will extend to include the receipt and disbursement of funds, including payrolls and payroll records.

Cost Accounting Systems

Developing and installing systems used primarily to determine the cost of producing a product or service and to measure the extent to which actual costs differ from those expected.

Budgeting Systems

Developing and installing systems used to forecast the financial results of future periods (year or month, etc.) and to provide a basis for planning, and for evaluating the results of operations. Like accounting and cost accounting, budgeting is used to provide information helpful in controlling costs.

Cash Forecasting

Developing and installing systems used to forecast the availability of cash. Like budgeting, cash forecasting is based upon the expected results of future activities, taking into account their effect on cash—collection of accounts receivable, payment for fixed assets acquired, etc.

Financial Feasibility Studies

Determining the expected revenues and disbursements associated with adding or acquiring a facility, and the financial effect on the organization of these expected revenues and disbursements.

PERSONNEL

Job Evaluation

Developing a system to evaluate and rate each position in terms of its requirements—education, experience, responsibility, manual and mental effort, etc. This evaluation is usually used as the basis for establishing wage and salary rates.

Wage and Salary Administration

This covers the broad field of job evaluation and compensation. It includes systems of merit rating, promotions employee benefits, and supplementary compensation; such as bonuses, stock options, and deferred compensation.

Personnel Record Keeping

Evaluating, and recommending needed improvements in, personnel records to assure information needed for compensating, evaluating, promoting, and terminating employees; for employee benefit programs; and for complying with Federal, local and union requirements.

Staff Training

Developing, carrying out, and installing systems of staff training adequate to provide employees with skills needed in their present positions and to prepare them for advancement to higher positions, to accommodate expected changes in operations and to generally improve the understanding, knowledge, and capabilities of employees.

Labor Relations

Training people to deal with employees and employees' unions in a considerate and equitable manner without prejudicing the rights and interests of the employer. Oftentimes, this will extend to assisting the employer in his negotiations with the union, and even in some cases, assisting the union in negotiating with the employer.

EDP

Computer Surveys

Studies to determine how well the computer and the entire EDP function is being utilized. This can include the applications of the computer; its systems, systems documentation, and programming; security against error and physical damage of the computer records and equipment; and general organization and utilization of EDP and related people.

Feasibility Studies

Studies to determine the costs and benefits expected from putting certain systems on a computer; or to determine if all the potential applications taken together justify a computer on premises, or use of someone else's equipment—service bureau or time-sharing.

Equipment Selection

Assisting the client to make a selection from the types of equipment available and the vendors offering it. Factors considered include: capability, availability, programs available, service, backup, and price.

Systems Development

Assisting in designing and installing systems for specific applications to be put on the computer. This can include determining system requirements, developing the system in concept, getting it approved, and designing it in detail, as well as helping to install it.

Computer Programming

Converting systems into computer program language so that the system can be run on the computer. The programs may be special purpose (designed to fit one user), or they may be general purpose (capable of being used by, and sold to, many users).

Computer Scheduling

Determining the most effective means of scheduling one or more programs on a computer to make maximum use of the central processing unit and peripheral equipment. Often this is done by using an electronic probe to determine the extent to which the central processing unit is used while the computer is processing, simultaneously, more than one program.

Employee Training

Training all levels of EDP people in skills related to their jobs—or jobs above them, in new equipment and new applications; and training managers in improved managerial techniques.

COST REDUCTION

Systems Analysis

Analyzing systems and other operations, to determine their necessity and effectiveness, with a view toward eliminating all or part of the system.

Work Simplification

Analyzing specific operations performed on a system, to eliminate the operation or to make it easier.

Work Measurement

Measuring the time required to perform a task, to permit improved scheduling of work and appraisal of workers' performance.

Incentive Compensation

Developing and installing systems of paying extra compensation to workers who perform more than the expected quantity of work during a given period of time.

SPECIAL SERVICES

Management Science—Training

Training people in the use of mathematical models and other techniques used in management science, and in how to recognize problems that lend themselves to this kind of solution, and in the various techniques available for each.

Management Science—Applications

Developing and installing a management science system to provide needed answers to a problem.

Telecommunications

Studying the use of telecommunication facilities for carrying messages and data between locations; and developing recommendations for the equipment, carriers, and circuits used to gather, transmit, switch, and deliver them.

Environmental Controls

Assisting clients to comply with laws and regulations governing the discharge of wastes. This can take the form of researching and interpreting laws and regulations, developing and/or recommending specific devices needed, and assisting in their proper installation.

Transportation—Analysis

Determining the best modes of transportation to use in moving products from one location to another. This can extend to obtaining needed freight classifications and rates, and to determining the optimum locations of warehouses and other distribution aids.

Transportation—Scheduling

Determining how best to schedule vehicles to reach desired points with the least amount of time and expense. Scheduling of route trucks is an example.

Resource Utilization

Determining how best to use a scarce and limiting resource (such as cash, a scarce material, or critical machine) in a way that will maximize profit. Using the resource to produce only high-markup items would be an example. This technique is usually employed in a complex situation where there are many trade-offs.

Index

Academicians
  methods of practice, 34
  role in the profession, 22
  types of practitioners, 30
American Institute of Certified Public Accountants (AICPA)
  consultants developing a data retrieval system, 48
  ethical restraints on practice development, 71
Assistance from client, consultant's, 52
Association of Consulting Management Engineers (ACME)
  definition of consulting, 6
  ethical restraints on practice development, 70
  involvement in executive search, 101
  size of profession, estimates, 23
  types of practitioners, 30

Billing engagements
  progress billing, 96
  timing of bills, 97
Booz, Allen & Hamilton
  range of practice, 31
  "sale of stock" to public, 31
  volume of business, 23
Building a consulting staff, 114
  background and training, 119
  career goals, 121
  consulting experience, 116
  personal characteristics, 115
  proper staffing, 122

Consultants News, volumes of billings by CPA firms, 23
CPA firms
  "Big Eight," classification of consulting work, 23
  entry into executive search, 40
  involvement in executive search, 101
  movement into consulting, 33
  types of practitioners, 30
  volume of business, 23

Cresap, McCormick and Paget
  captive firms, 32
  membership in ACME, 32
  ownership by First National City Corp., 32

Development of a consulting practice, 70
  ethical and legal considerations, 71

EDP equipment manufacturers
  entry into the profession, range of practice, 38
  types of practitioners, 30
Engagements—executive search, 101
  billing, 112
  concluding arrangements, 111
  conducting search, 106
    defining the position, 106
    sources of information on candidates, 107
  obtaining engagements, 104
  practice development, 103
  presenting candidates, 110
Engagements—survey on system type
  billing, 96
  carrying out, 84
  follow-up, 98
  obtaining, 75
  organizing, 80
Executive search
  origin of practicing firms, 40
  relationship to other types of consulting, 41
  types of firms practicing, 40, 101
Executive search firms
  origin, 40
  range of practice, 40

First National City Corp., ownership of Cresap, McCormick and Paget, 32
Foreign market, the, 124
  future, 135
  location of the market, 126
  nature of the market, 127
  supplying the market, 130
Fry Consultants, types of practice, 31
Future of consulting, the, 137
  consulting opportunities
    EDP, 138
    government, 138
    service industries, 138
  services available
    outside objectivity, 137
    specialized knowhow, 137, 139

summary, 140
valuable disciplines, 139

Government, volume and types of consulting work done, 46

Heidrick and Struggles, entry into executive search, 40

Industry, volume and types of consulting received, 42
In-house consultants
    number of companies having, 24
    types of practitioners, 30
Institute of Management Consultants (IMC), ethical restraints on practice development, 70
Institutions, volume and types of consulting received, 47

Kearney, A. T., types of practice, 31

Little, A. D., types of practice, 31

Management consulting
    building a consulting staff, 114
        background and training, 119
        career goals, 121
        consulting experience, 116
        personal characteristics, 115
        proper staffing, 122
    conduct of the practice
        analyzing information and developing recommendations, 92
        billing engagements, 96
        carrying out engagements, 84
        developing the report (or system), 92
        following up on engagements, 98
        obtaining information, 87
        organizing engagements, 80
        practice development, 70
        securing engagements, 75
            proposal letters, 75
            requests for proposals, 75
    definition, 6
    evolution
        Cold War, 16
        computer era, 18
        factors favoring growth, 124
        Korean War, 15
        origin, 13
        World War I, 14
        World War II, 15
    executive search engagements, 101
        billing engagements, 112

Management consulting (*Continued*)
  executive search engagements (*Continued*)
    concluding arrangements, 111
    conducting searches, 106
    obtaining engagements, 104
    practice development, 103
    presenting candidates, 110
  foreign market, 124
    future, the, 135
    location of the market, 126
    nature of the market, 127
      developed nations, 127
      developing nations, 128
    opportunities (past) for American firms, 125
    supplying the market, 130
      collecting and converting the fee, 134
      obtaining the work, 131
      performing the engagement, 133
  future of consulting, the, 137
    EDP, 138
    government, 138
    industry, 137
    service industries, 138
    services requiring outside objectivity, 137
    services requiring specialized knowhow, 137, 139
    summary, 140
    valuable disciplines, 139
    value of knowledge of newer disciplines, 141
  range of services, 25
    factors affecting type of service demanded, 27
    functions and activities, 26
  selecting clients, 50
    potential danger signals, 54
    requirements for a successful engagement, 50
  selecting consultants, 59
    factors to consider, 60
    methods of selection, 79
  size of practice, 21
    classifying work as consulting, 22
    dollar volume, 23
    number of firms, 23
    number of professionals, 23
  types of clients
    government, 46
    industry, 42
    institutions, 47
  types of practitioners, 30
    academicians, 34
    CPA firms, 33

58719

    EDP equipment manufacturers, 38
    executive search, 40
    in-house consultants, 36
    management consulting firms, 31
    software firms, 38
    sole practitioners, 35
  types of services, 6
Manufacturing, volume and types of consulting work done, 43
McKinsey and Company
  range of practice, 31
  volume of business, 23

Objective appraisal, 7

Project assistance, 10
Proposals
  contents, 77
  how used, 75

Religious organizations, work done for them by consultants, 48
Reports
  outlines, 94
  quality, 93
  style, 95
  types, 93
Requests for proposals, 75
Requirements for a successful engagement, 50

Securities and Exchange Commission (SEC), product line reporting, 33
Selecting consultants, factors to consider, 60
Service industries, volume and types of consulting work done, 44
Software firms
  entry into the profession—range of practice, 38
  types of practitioners, 30
Sole practitioners
  mode of operation, 35
  types of practitioners, 30
Spencer Stuart & Associates, entry into executive search, 40

Technical knowhow, 9
Trade, volume and types of consulting work done, 43